Understanding
SAMUEL BECKETT

UNDERSTANDING MODERN
EUROPEAN and LATIN AMERICAN
LITERATURE

JAMES HARDIN, *SERIES EDITOR*

ADVISORY BOARD

* * * * *

Understanding Günter Grass
by Alan Frank Keele

Understanding Graciliano Ramos
by Celso Lemos de Oliveira

Understanding Gabriel García Márquez
by Kathleen McNerney

Understanding Claude Simon
by Ralph Sarkonak

Understanding Mario Vargas Llosa
by Sara Castro-Klarén

Understanding Samuel Beckett
by Alan Astro

Understanding Jean-Paul Sartre
by Philip R. Wood

Understanding Albert Camus
by David R. Ellison

UNDERSTANDING

SAMUEL
BECKETT

by ALAN ASTRO

UNIVERSITY OF SOUTH CAROLINA PRESS

Copyright © University of South Carolina 1990

Published in Columbia, South Carolina, by the
University of South Carolina Press

Manufactured in the United States of America

Library of Congress Cataloging-in-Publication Data

Astro, Alan.
    Understanding Samuel Beckett / by Alan Astro.
        p.   cm. — (Understanding modern European and Latin
    American literature)
    Includes bibliographical references.
    ISBN 0–87249–686–4
    1. Beckett, Samuel, 1906–1989   —Criticism and interpretation.
I. Title.   II. Series.
PR6003.E282Z5637   1990
848′.91409—dc20   89–70759
                                                          CIP

Understanding *Endgame* can only be understanding why it cannot be understood. . . .

—Theodor Adorno, "Towards an Understanding of *Endgame*"

And I said, with rapture, Here is something I can study all my life, and never understand.

—Samuel Beckett, *Molloy*

CONTENTS

EDITOR'S PREFACE

Understanding Modern European and Latin American Literature has been planned as a series of guides for undergraduate and graduate students and nonacademic readers. Like its companion series, *Understanding Contemporary American Literature,* the aim of the books is to provide an introduction to the life and writings of prominent modern authors and to explicate their most important works.

Modern literature makes special demands, and this is particularly true of foreign literature, in which the reader must contend not only with unfamiliar, often arcane artistic conventions and philosophical concepts, but also with the handicap of reading the literature in translation. It is a truism that the nuances of one language can be rendered in another only imperfectly (and this problem is especially acute in fiction), but the fact that the works of European and Latin American writers are situated in a historical and cultural setting quite different from our own can be as great a hindrance to the understanding of these works as the linguistic barrier. For this reason, the UMELL series emphasizes the sociological and historical background of the writers treated. The peculiar philosophical and cultural traditions of a given culture may be particularly important for an understanding of certain authors, and these will be taken up in the introductory chapter and also in the discussion of those works to which this information is relevant. Beyond this, the books will treat the specifically literary aspects of the author under discussion and attempt to explain the complexities of contemporary literature lucidly. The books are conceived as introductions to the authors covered, not as comprehensive analyses. They do not provide detailed summaries of plot since they are meant to be used in conjunction with the books they treat, not as a substitute for the study of the original works. It is our hope that the UMELL series will help to increase knowledge and understanding of the European and Latin American cultures and will serve to make the literature of those cultures more accessible.

Professor Astro's *Understanding Samuel Beckett* fills the need for an up-to-date, comprehensive study in English of a Nobel Prize winner in literature (1969) who uniquely belongs both to Irish and to French literary traditions. Although Beckett has become a part of the American cultural consciousness—largely by virtue of his play *Waiting for Godot* (1952)—his other works have, relatively speaking, been neglected in recent years. The present volume traces the techniques, themes, and linguistic concerns of Beckett's works from the 1930s through his latest works and attempts to show their relationship one to the other.

J. H.

A computer check at a major research library in the United States turns up over two hundred volumes with the name Beckett in their titles. A new book on the subject could hardly be totally original, but *Understanding Samuel Beckett* attempts to do something other than repeat the works that preceded it. Its aim is to introduce Beckett to the nonspecialist reader while treating specific concerns that do not always receive the attention they deserve: the author's bilingualism, the psychoanalytic texture of his works, and the narrative impasse he exploits through the use of the first-person pronoun.

My indebtedness to those who have gone before me will be evident to any Beckett scholar, but it seemed contrary to the introductory nature of this series to encumber the pages with references to previous studies. Instead, the bibliography lists the works that were most useful. I supply footnotes in cases where a particular writer has devised a truly novel interpretation or brought in exceptionally interesting information.

I must acknowledge my great fortune in having been able to interview Samuel Beckett. The recently deceased Elmar Tophoven, Beckett's German translator, graciously arranged the meeting and shared with me his experiences in translating Beckett.

My debt is equally great toward my professors, especially Charles Porter of Yale University and Josué

Harari of Johns Hopkins University, whose support and encouragement have been invaluable. I am also grateful to James Hardin, of the University of South Carolina, for his comments on my manuscript, and to David Caffry, of the University of South Carolina Press, for his patience. And I warmly thank my colleagues at the Department of Foreign Languages at Trinity University, who more than colleagues have shown themselves to be, time and again, true friends.

As always, I have benefited from the encouragement of my parents, Simmie and Paul Astro, and my aunt, Anne Roseman. My friends Catherine Colardelle and Peter Joffe provided much needed support by commenting on a draft of the first chapters. Salim Jay never let me forget the necessity to continue working, and Glenn Swiadon gave me endless encouragement, no matter the cost. Finally, David Jacobson was of great help in checking proofs.

ABBREVIATIONS

Beckett's works in English will be referred to by the following abbreviations; page numbers correspond to the editions cited in the bibliography. Beckett's French texts will be referred to by their full titles.

Since Beckett's work occasionally contains ellipses in the original, ellipses indicating omissions of the text will appear in brackets.

C	*Company*
CP	*Collected Poems in English and French*
CSP	*Collected Shorter Plays of Samuel Beckett*
CSPR	*Collected Shorter Prose 1945–1980*
D	*Disjecta*
E	*Endgame*
F	*Fizzles*
FL	*First Love*
H	*How It Is*
HD	*Happy Days*
ISIS	*Ill Seen Ill Said*
M	*Murphy*
MC	*Mercier and Camier*
MPTK	*More Pricks than Kicks*
P	*Proust*
STN	*Stories and Texts for Nothing*

ABBREVIATIONS

TN	*Three Novels by Samuel Beckett: Molloy, Malone Dies, The Unnamable*
W	*Watt*
WFG	*Waiting for Godot*
WH	*Worstward Ho*

CHRONOLOGY

1906	Born in Foxrock, Ireland, a suburb of Dublin, to an upper-middle-class Protestant family, on Good Friday, April 13. By Beckett's own account, his childhood is happy.
1911–23	Attends Irish day and boarding schools.
1923–27	Studies French and Italian at Trinity College in Dublin.
1928–30	In Paris, *lecteur* of English at the Ecole Normale Supérieure. Writes his first poems, in English. Meets James Joyce and publishes a critical piece, "Dante ... Bruno. Vico. . Joyce," on Joyce's *Work in Progress,* which will become *Finnegans Wake.* Also writes his monograph on the French author Marcel Proust.
1930–32	Back in Dublin, assistant in French at Trinity.
1932	Leaves teaching to devote himself fully to writing.
1933	Writes *More Pricks than Kicks,* a collection of short stories loosely tied together into a novel.
1935	In London, writes the novel *Murphy.*
1936–37	Travels extensively through Germany, and then settles in Paris.

1938–40   Writes poems in French and English, and translates *Murphy* into French.

1940–42   Active in the French resistance against the Nazi occupation.

1942–45   Beckett's resistance group having been discovered by the Gestapo, he escapes to a village in the south of France. He does farm work and writes *Watt,* in English.

1946–50   Returns to Paris. In a productive spurt, writes in French most of his best-known works: the play *En attendant Godot (Waiting for Godot)* and the novels *Molloy, Malone meurt,* and *L'Innommable (Molloy, Malone Dies,* and *The Unnamable).* These texts will all be published by 1953.

1953–56   *Waiting for Godot* premieres in Paris on 5 January 1953. Beckett is deeply involved in translation of his own works into English, as well as writing new ones.

1957   *All That Fall,* a radio play that Beckett wrote in English, is aired by the BBC on January 13. The play *Fin de partie (Endgame)* premieres in the original French in London on April 3.

1958   Premiere of *Krapp's Last Tape,* a play written in English, in London, on October 28.

1961   Publication of the French original of the novel *Comment c'est (How It Is). Happy Days,* a play written in English, opens in

New York. Beckett shares the International Publishers' Prize with the Argentine writer Jorge Luis Borges.

After 1961 Beckett stops publishing longer works, but he will write over forty shorter dramatic and prose pieces. Included below are only those discussed at length in this study.

1963 *Play* debuts in German translation at Ulm, West Germany, on June 14; the English original will open the following year in London on April 7.

1964 Supervises the making of *Film* in New York.

1965 Publishes the prose piece *Imagination morte imaginez (Imagination Dead Imagine)*.

1966 First piece for television, *Eh Joe,* is aired in translation by a West German station on April 13, and in the English original by the BBC on July 4. Publication of the prose piece *Bing* (in French, translated into English as *Ping*).

1969 Beckett receives the Nobel Prize for Literature. Publishes the prose piece *Sans,* which appears in English the next year as *Lessness*. The play *Breath* premieres in New York on June 16.

1972 *Not I* premieres in New York on November 22.

1976 Publication of the prose piece *Pour en finir encore (For to End Yet Again)*.

1977	*Ghost Trio* televised on the BBC, April 17.
1980	Publication of *Company,* a prose text in English.
1981	*Quad,* a nonverbal dance/mime piece, is broadcast by a West German station on October 8.
1983	Publication of *Worstward Ho,* a short prose in English.
1988	*Stirrings Still*, a prose text, is published.
1989	Beckett dies in Paris on December 22.

Understanding
SAMUEL BECKETT

CHAPTER ONE

Overview

Some months before Samuel Beckett's death on 22 December 1989, a story was circulating in Paris. An elderly woman points out an old gentleman she has sighted. "That's Samuel Beckett," she says to a friend, "the author of *Waiting for Godot*." Beckett, whose hearing is more acute than she presumes, answers from afar: "Yes, and I am still waiting." If this anecdote is true, it shows that at well over eighty Beckett had lost none of his wit. Like his characters who spend an entire play waiting for a Mr. Godot who never comes, Beckett would have been looking toward a meeting also to be missed: the encounter with death. For when we die, we do not recognize death; we are dead to it when it has arrived.

The statement attributed to Beckett is of a piece with voices in his works. A novel he wrote in 1948 begins, "I shall soon be quite dead at last," and a story from two years earlier starts off, "I don't know when I died" (TN 179, STN 27). It seems as though Beckett had wanted to narrate his own death for a long time. The voice that would speak us us from beyond is strange in another sense: Beckett wrote in a foreign language. This Irishman started out as a writer in English, but he composed his best-known works in French. They are the plays *En attendant Godot* (1952, translated as *Waiting for Godot*) and *Fin de partie* (1957, *Endgame*), and the trilogy made up of the novels *Molloy* (1951, *Molloy*),

Malone meurt (1951, *Malone Dies*), and *L'Innommable* (1953, *The Unnamable*).

Beckett is certainly not the only author to have written in a language other than his native one. For centuries poets and philosophers used Latin rather than the commonly spoken language; even Dante, whose *Divine Comedy* was the first major poetic work in Italian, defended the vernacular in a Latin treatise, *De vulgari eloquentia* (1304–06, "On the Eloquence of the Vulgar"). In modern times writers using foreign tongues are rarer. Joseph Conrad, a Pole, and Vladimir Nabokov, a Russian, adopted English; and Eugène Ionesco, a Rumanian, wrote in French. Yet as theater critic Martin Esslin has noted, the situation of these writers is different from Beckett's. They chose languages with larger audiences than those of their mother tongues, whereas Beckett abandoned English, the most widely used idiom in this century.[1] Also, the other writers had intense contact with their second languages from the earliest age: Ionesco's mother was French, and he spent part of his childhood in France; Nabokov learned English thoroughly as a child from governesses and tutors; and Conrad's father, a translator, would teach him English. Contrarily, Beckett's first acquaintance with French occurred where most of us learn a foreign language: in school.

Thus Beckett, born on 13 April 1906 in Foxrock, near Dublin, received instruction in French in the same places as other scions of middle-class Irish Protestant families: at a preparatory day school in Dublin and at a boarding school in Northern Ireland. Beckett continued his French studies with great success at Dublin's Trinity College. After graduation he was *lecteur* of English for the years 1928–30 at the Ecole Normale Supérieure in Paris, a school at which the future philosopher Jean-Paul Sartre had just finished studying when Beckett arrived. In 1930 Beckett returned to Dublin to serve for two years as assistant in French at Trinity, after which he left teaching to devote himself to writing. In 1933 he composed, in English, a collection of stories called *More Pricks than Kicks,* and in London in 1935 he wrote a novel in English entitled *Murphy.* He then traveled through Germany before settling in Paris in 1937. There Beckett wrote some poetry in French, but he returned to English for his next novel. This was *Watt,* published in 1953 but written during the war as Beckett hid in the French countryside, his life endangered because of the role he had played in the resistance against the Nazi occupation. After the war Beckett started writing exclusively in French, and composed nothing new in English until the radio play *All That Fall,* aired in 1957. He wrote thereafter in both his native and adopted languages, and he translated—usually by himself, sometimes in collaboration—his French texts into English and vice versa.

These two languages do not exhaust Beckett's repertoire. He also studied Italian at Trinity, and the first story of his first book, "Dante and the Lobster" in *More Pricks than Kicks,* begins with an Italian lesson. (References to Dante abound in Beckett's work, and the impasses in which his heroes find themselves can be seen as reworkings of Dante's hell and purgatory.[2]) Beckett also picked up enough Spanish to translate a volume of Mexican poetry for UNESCO,[3] and his travels in the 1930s gave him ample opportunity to perfect his German. Later on, he would direct his own plays in Berlin, and he would meticulously check the German versions of his works prepared by Elmar Tophoven, who even suspected Beckett of having written some texts in German and consigning them to oblivion.[4]

Beckett's affection for other languages becomes less surprising when we consider that for the Irish generally, English is somewhat foreign. Their ancestral language, Gaelic, is mostly spoken by older people in rural areas, though in an effort to keep it alive various organizations cultivate it and by law it appears on all official documents. Thus English, the native language of the majority of the Irish, is nonetheless felt to be a foreign tongue imposed on them by the British colonizer, from whom they only achieved independence in 1921 and against whom hostility still rages in Northern Ireland. Sartre said that the French, by educating their colonial subjects in their language, installed themselves as permanent mediators in the most intimate exchanges among Africans;[5] the same is true of the English-speaking Irish, who could say, along with the narrator of Beckett's *Unnamable,* that they are "stranger[s] in [their] own midst, surrounded by invaders" (TN 396).

Despite the distance Beckett took from English by writing in French, he demonstrated little sympathy for the nationalist attempt to revive Gaelic. In *Molloy* he has the narrator say, "Tears and laughter, they are so much Gaelic to me" (TN 37). By parodying the expression "That's all Greek to me," he consigns Gaelic to the irremediably incomprehensible; yet what makes Gaelic impossible to understand is not only its distance but its intimacy. Like "tears and laughter," the affect that the Gaelic language conveys cannot be put into meaningful words. Many descendants of those who spoke

Gaelic know it only in fragmentary form: isolated words or expressions, of whose meaning they may be totally unconscious, can become laden with emotion as the bearers of a past they are cut off from. In this way Gaelic, supposedly a dead language, remains alive.

Likewise a dialogue in Beckett's *All That Fall* suggests in what way a living language—English—is dead:

Mrs. Rooney:	No, no, I am agog, tell me all, then we shall press on and never pause, never pause, till we come safe to haven. *(Pause.)*
Mr. Rooney:	Never pause ... safe to haven ... Do you know, Maddy, sometimes one would think you were struggling with a dead language.
Mrs. Rooney:	Yes indeed, Dan, I know full well what you mean, I often have that feeling, it is unspeakably excruciating.
Mr. Rooney:	I confess I have it sometimes myself, when I happen to overhear what I am saying.
Mrs. Rooney:	Well, you know, it will be dead in time, just like our own poor dear Gaelic, there is that to be said (CSP 34).

We must understand Mrs. Rooney's words metaphorically. She is not suggesting that English will someday be replaced by the language of a greater empire, as Gaelic gave way to the British conquerors. Rather, English is dead as any language is when we "overhear" our words, as Mr. Rooney puts it. Literally *over*-hearing what we say, listening to it with extreme attention, we must ask ourselves how the acoustic matter that words are manages to convey sense.

The dissolution of the link between the sound of a word and its meaning appears clearly in a passage from Beckett's *Watt:*

Looking at a pot, for example, or thinking of a pot, at one of Mr. Knott's pots, of one of Mr Knott's pots, it was in vain that Watt said, Pot, pot. [...] For the pot remained a pot, Watt felt sure of that, for everyone but Watt. For Watt alone it was not a pot, any more (w 81–82).

Although Watt believes that the pot is still one for all but himself, he has temporarily robbed the word of its meaning for us as well by repeating it and rhyming it with Watt and Knott. Thus we begin to understand why Beckett has claimed, "My work is a matter of fundamental sounds";[6] as his character Molloy says, his words tend to become "pure sounds, free of all meaning" (TN 50).

For Beckett, writing does not invest words with sense but rather strips them of it, which gives us insight into his decision to write in a foreign language. No matter how well we come to know the tongue of another nation, the words always seem more arbitrary than ours, the link between sound and meaning less self-evident. The questionable command of a language by even the best foreign speaker is mimicked by Beckett in one of the reasons he has given for writing in French: "Pour faire remarquer moi," *to call attention to myself,* or, more literally, *to call attention me.*[7] Beckett's French here was glaringly, and intentionally, incorrect: the proper form would be "Pour me faire remarquer."

Beckett offered other explanations for choosing French, which suggest it represented a kind of asceticism. He said the use of a second language allowed him to "impoverish" or "weaken" himself, and write without "style" or "poetry."[8] Thus Beckett's French is anything but the classical literary language of such writers as André Gide or Marcel Proust. His is a manner at once conversational and laborious, as in this passage where Molloy speaks of the widow Lousse's parrot:

Elle avait un perroquet, très joli, toutes les couleurs les plus appréciées. Je le comprenais mieux que sa maîtresse. Je ne veux pas dire que je le comprenais mieux qu'elle ne le comprenait, je veux dire que je le comprenais mieux que je ne la comprenais elle (*Molloy* 49).

Or in the English version, prepared by Beckett in collaboration with Patrick Bowles:

She had a parrot, very pretty, all the most approved colours. I understood him better than his mistress. I don't mean I understood him better than she understood him, I mean I understood him better than I understood her (TN 37).

Beckett also explained his use of French by saying that in *Watt* English was "running away" with him;[9] unlike Watt, who compulsively repeats the word *pot*, Molloy at least makes the pretense of controlling his words. The passage above is an excellent example of what critic Jean-Michel Rey calls Beckett's "attention to the slightest particles of the language," which makes his French uncanny: "Samuel Beckett forces us . . . to learn to read our language all over again. . . . [He] works on the very matter of the French language in memory of English . . . : immense detour at whose end our language is capable of surprising us, of returning to us in an unforeseen form. Beckett's 'dialect' disarms us."[10] Thus Beckett's French functions as a kind of foreign language within French.

It could be argued that the English translation of the passage on Molloy's parrot is not as aberrant as the original; the French pride themselves on the clarity of their language, and Molloy's gleeful emphasis on muddy syntax seems peculiarly transgressive. Yet Beckett has said he could return to English because French had taught him how to write less expansively; a good example is this quotation from his recent prose work *Company* (1980):

Use of the second person marks the voice. That of the third that cankerous other. Could he speak to and of whom the voice speaks there would be a first. But he cannot. He shall not. You cannot. You shall not. (C 8).

The narrator here is reduced to conjugation. This passage makes it clear that if Beckett's French seems slightly foreign to native speakers, the same is true of his English.

Molloy's parrot is an excellent emblem for the foreignness of language, since we imagine that these birds remain unaware of the message they are emitting. They speak words as pure acoustic matter, as "fundamental sounds": hence the irony of Molloy's understanding the parrot, whereas the parrot does not understand its own words. Parrots turn up as well in other works by Beckett: *Murphy* (M 39), *Watt* (W 156), *Mercier and Camier* (MC 27, 28, 36, 121), *Texts for Nothing* (STN 108), *Malone Dies* (TN 218), and *The Unnamable* (TN 335). For example, in the last text the narrator says of his own endless talking: "A parrot, that's what they're up against, a parrot." In the original this sentence reads, "Un perroquet, ils sont tombés sur un bec de perroquet," which literally translated means *A parrot, they've fallen upon a parrot's beak*. Thus the French contains the word for "beak," which is *bec,* as in *Bec*kett; this name, which resonates in French as "little beak," attests to our author's descent from French Huguenots who took refuge in Ireland in the late seventeenth century. Beckett's ancestry— and the fact that in French his name evokes an organ of speech—may have unconsciously motivated his desire to write in that language.

The parrots in Beckett not only allude to his name; they also symbolize the repetitiousness of his work. For example, the second half of *Waiting for Godot* presents much of the same action as the first, and the characters affirm time and again that they are "waiting for Godot"; in *Happy Days* (1961) a woman buried in sand says on several occasions, "This will have been [*or* is going to be] a happy day"; Beckett's play entitled *Play* (1963) consists of two cycles of the same words spoken by the same characters.

Repetition is not only a technique in Beckett; it is also a theme, which means that repetition is spoken of repeatedly. Thus we read in his 1961 novel *Comment c'est (How It Is),* "He sings yes always the same song pause SAME SONG" (H 97), words that echo what the

9

narrator of the story *L'Expulsé* (1946, *The Expelled*) had said of any tale he could possibly tell: "You will see how alike they are" (STN 25). The narrator of *The Unnamable* admits "all things here recur sooner or later" (TN 299), and these sentences from *Company* characterize Beckett's oeuvre as a whole: "Another trait is repetitiousness. Repeatedly with only minor variants the same bygone" (C 16).

A generalized compulsion to repeat was posited by Freud in his 1920 work *Beyond the Pleasure Principle*. As an example he points out that while adults may believe "novelty is always the condition of enjoyment," for children it is otherwise: "if a child has been told a nice story, he will insist on hearing it over and over again rather than a new one; and he will remorselessly stipulate that the repetition shall be an identical one."[11] The narrator of Beckett's *Textes pour rien* (1955, *Texts for Nothing*) recalls that in his childhood he would have his father tell him, "evening after evening, the same old story I knew by heart" (STN 79), but Beckett's art consists in his ability to repeat, time and again, the same thing while providing the novelty that is the condition for enjoyment. His texts may seem interchangeable on the level of *what is said,* but the *way it is said* is always different. An example is the structure of the novel *Mercier et Camier (Mercier and Camier,* written in 1946 but not published until 1970). In the original French every third chapter consists of an eccentric outline of the preceding two, mentioning the most curious details while neglecting the pivots of the plot. *The Unnamable* offers an explanation for such repetition with variations: "They always repeat the same thing, the same old litany [. . .], they'd do better to think of what

10

they're saying, in order at least to vary its presentation" (TN 374).

It could appear that Beckett's insistence on translating his own writings partakes of his tendency to say the same thing a bit differently. However, this poses a problem: translating a text is usually seen as recasting its sense into new words, but if Beckett's work tends toward destruction of sense, there would be nothing left to translate. Or it would seem contrary to the movement of Beckett's writings to recuperate sense through translation.

In "The Task of the Translator" the German literary theoretician Walter Benjamin offered a view of translation as something other than the retransmission of the meaning of the original.[12] What is translated, said Benjamin, is not the sense but the impact of the text on its language. We have seen how Beckett's English comes to resemble his French by doing violence to English usage; this violence is figured in Beckett's description of his own activity as "the wastes and wilds of self-translation,"[13] and in threats uttered in *The Unnamable:* "I'll fix their gibberish for them"; "I'll fix their jargon for them" (TN 324–25, 326).

The language of the others may be "gibberish" or "jargon," but it is all the Unnamable has: "I have no language but theirs" (TN 325). It is also all he is: "I'm in words, made of words, others' words [...], I'm all these words, all these strangers" (TN 386). In the original French this last phrase reads, "Je suis tous ces mots, tous ces étrangers," which can be translated as *I'm all these words, all these foreigners.*

The otherness of the self within language, the constitution of the self by a necessarily foreign idiom, shows

11

how much Beckett's writing is in consonance with the theories of the French psychoanalyst Jacques Lacan. Lacan emphasizes that the child, acceding to the realm of language, assumes the name that others have given him and inserts himself into a symbolic system not of his own making.[14] Likewise, the Unnamable's alienation from speech goes beyond any distinction between native and foreign languages:

> All solicit me in the same tongue, the only one they taught me. They told me there were others, I don't regret not knowing them. The moment silence is broken in this way it can only mean one thing (TN 336–37).

Or as Clov says to Hamm in *Endgame:* "I use the words you taught me. If they don't mean anything any more, teach me others. Or let me be silent" (E 44).

Paradoxically, translation partially realizes the desire for silence. Since what can be said in one language cannot necessarily be said in another, translating a text entails deciding what of it *not* to translate, what of it will be suppressed. Silencing is also part of *writing* in a foreign language. Beckett chose to write in French not because he could say more in French than in English, or because he could say something different in French than in English, but because, like anyone who uses a foreign language, he would say *less* in French than in English. But how can this "lessness"—to use the title of a short prose work by Beckett—be reconciled with the repetitiousness that characterizes his oeuvre?

The Unnamable provides a solution. He desires

silence but keeps it at bay, so that it may be savored all the more when it finally arrives:

> However that may be I think I'll soon go silent for good, in spite of its being prohibited. Then, yes, phut, just like that, just like one of the living, then I'll be dead, I think I'll soon be dead, I hope I find it a change. I should have liked to go silent first, there were moments I thought that would be my reward for having spoken so long and so valiantly, to enter living into silence, so as to be able to enjoy it, no (TN 396).

Beckett's insistence on translating himself partakes of the dialectic between the desire for silence and the compulsion to repeat. By suppressing as well as repeating, his translations in their own way realize, and yet delay, the silence longed for in his works.

Another way Beckett's writings put off silence is by constantly commenting upon themselves, an aspect of his work we may call metatheatrical or metanarrative, depending on whether the work involved is dramatic or novelistic. This self-commentary seems at times to preempt whatever could possibly be said about this author. Before we have a chance to remark that it is paradoxical that Beckett speaks of a desire for silence that his very speech interrupts, the Unnamable has already admitted that "silence [...] does not appear to have been very conspicuous up to now" (TN 388–89). Likewise, we have seen how Beckett's narrators save us the trouble of pointing out their repetitiousness. Is one beginning to feel that such writing is pointless? Vladimir in *Waiting for Godot* has already said, "This is becoming really insignificant" (WFG 44). Do you find yourself tired of Beckett's senseless writing and wish you were through with it? Hamm and Clov in *Endgame* feel the same way: "Enough, it's time it ended." "Have you not finished? Will you never finish? Will this never finish?" (E 3, 23). And if you are reading this book because you have been assigned a paper on Beckett and are at a loss what to say, your situation too has been anticipated by Beckett. For narrators in the trilogy speak of writing as a "pensum," a rote assignment imposed upon misbehaving schoolchildren (TN 32, 310, 311; *Malone meurt* 25).

All that can be said about Beckett's work seems to have already been written in it. We find ourselves at an interpretive impasse, just as his characters are often at an existential impasse. Yet this critical impasse has turned out to be extremely fruitful. Beckett is among the contemporary authors who have received the greatest critical attention. Likewise, the existential impasse has been a very rich source for theater, from antiquity on.

For example, Sophocles' *Oedipus the King* begins with a plague at Thebes that will not cease until the assassin of the former king, Laius, is found. Oedipus is lodged between two impossible options: either he can follow his queen Jocasta's suggestion not to look for the murderer and let the plague rage; or he can search for the culprit, only to find out that he himself is the guilty one, that Laius was his father and Jocasta his mother. Similarly, in Shakespeare's play Hamlet must either please his mother and let the usurper of his father's throne rule; or he must avenge his father's death by killing his uncle, thereby himself committing regicide, a symbolic form of patricide.

Sartre's drama also exploited the impasses of classical tragedy in order to dramatize the tenets of existentialist philosophy. For example, in his *La P ... respectueuse* (1947, "The Respectful Whore"), a play set in the American South, a white prostitute finds herself before a choice made impossible by the conflict between the prevailing racism and the most basic morality. Either she must falsely accuse a black alleged to have raped her, or she must allow a white, who killed another black supposedly in her defense, to be seen as guilty of an unjustified murder.

The problem of choice is central to Sartre's plays, for his brand of existentialism accepts as a given the absence of God and the resultant lack of an external principle to guide our actions. Our existences have no previously assigned meaning: hence the absurdity of life. Yet Sartre argues that this meaninglessness can be counteracted by the exercise of choice: by deciding to act in a certain way, we define our lives and ourselves. Even if we do not believe we are choosing, we nonetheless choose by not choosing, by simply going along with the status quo. As Sartre says, we are "condemned to be free."[15]

Moreover, freedom is not absolute but is defined by the situation in which we find ourselves. The relevant situation for existentialism at its origin was the Nazi occupation of France. Sartre's plays, written during the war or shortly thereafter, reflect their historical moment by portraying characters who must choose between clear-cut alternatives, for one was either for or against collaboration with the German invader. Sartre has admitted that since the war political options have become more hazy—so hazy, some would argue, that one is at a loss to know what to do. Moreover, even if one becomes politically involved, it is clear that the kinds of choices that the existentialist places at the core of the human personality are not everyday occurrences. Rarely does one have the occasion to be a traitor to a cause or a champion of it. It is usually the absurdity of life that one is aware of—and not the possibility of exercising one's freedom so as to counteract the absurdity. Accordingly, during the war Beckett joined the Resistance and took a political stand that coincided with that of the existentialists, but since then he has remained almost totally nonpolitical. Beckett's characters are like Sartre's in having a profound sense of the absurdity of life, but they are incapable of mitigating the absurdity. Thus in *Waiting for Godot* the two main characters go on waiting faithfully for Godot, even after they begin to suspect that he may never come. The situation in *Endgame* is graver: four characters, who may be the last survivors of a nuclear holocaust, are not even afforded the luxury of waiting, for no one could possibly come. In comparison, the circumstance in which the protagonist in *Happy Days* finds herself may not seem so bad: she is merely buried in sand, first up to her waist and then up to her neck. These unlivable situations, which in an existentialist play would be treated tragically, are shown to be disturbingly comic. As Nell says in *Endgame,* "Nothing is funnier than unhappiness" (E 18).

Beckett's distance from existentialism as well as his indebtedness to it emerges most clearly in *Waiting for Godot.* The bareness of the plot and setting reminds us of Sartre's play *Huis clos* (1944, translated as *No Exit*), which depicts three characters in hell, condemned to spend eternity together in a room. As in *Godot,* theirs is a fruitless wait: being dead, they cannot be delivered by death. Yet they come to exist as a function of their present situation, because each is aware of the two others judging him or her. Thus when one of the characters is offered the chance to escape, he remains—so as to continue to exist in the others' eyes.

No Exit shows us the characters' first day in hell, when the heroic acceptance of their fate could be a meaningful act. The play would have been different— and quite humorous—if it showed them several years later, after they had gotten to know each other all too well and could predict each other's every word and movement. No act would express a free will capable of defining its agent but would simply occur through force of habit. The repertoire of gesture and language would have become exhausted, and the characters would be reduced to stock actions and phrases. Had Sartre let his inmates in hell live together long enough to reach this point, *No Exit* would have become *Waiting for Godot.*

In *Waiting for Godot* there is no possibility of achieving a meaningful existence through the present situation, for the present situation seems to have been going on since time immemorial and is defined only with respect to a future—the arrival of Godot—that will never materialize. Moreover, the main characters, Vladimir and Estragon, can no longer exist through the fact that they look at each other, because they have merged into each other. The two form what Beckett calls in *The Unnamable* a "pseudocouple" (TN 297)—

17

"pseudo" because they are hardly two people any more; like Don Quixote and Sancho Panza, or Laurel and Hardy, each one is unimaginable without the other. Pseudocouples in Beckett's work include Bim and Bom in *Murphy,* Sam and Watt in *Watt,* Pozzo and Lucky in *Waiting for Godot,* Hamm and Clov in *Endgame,* Mercier and Camier in *Mercier and Camier,* and Pim and Bom in *How It Is.* In Beckett's work the autonomous subject that forms the basis of existentialism is no longer to be found.

In *Godot* existence is denounced as simulacrum—"We always find something, eh Didi, to give us the impression we exist" (WFG 44)—as are choice and responsibility. For this is how Vladimir responds to the cry of another character for help:

To all mankind they were addressed, those cries for help still ringing in our ears! But at this place, at this moment of time, all mankind is us, whether we like it or not. Let us make the most of it, before it is too late! Let us represent worthily for once the foul brood to which a cruel fate consigned us! [...] It is true that when with folded arms we weigh the pros and cons we are no less a credit to our species. [...] What are we doing here, *that* is the question. And we are blessed in this, that we happen to know the answer. Yes, in this immense confusion one thing alone is clear. We are waiting for Godot to come—(WFG 51).

Vladimir's reasoning befits Sartre's man *en situation,* who is aware that his free will must be exercised in his present circumstances. Yet it is clear that the very act of taking time to discuss whether or not to help the man in trouble mitigates the usefulness of responding to his plea. The whole speech is rather self-congratulatory and has as its end product the ultimate alibi: we are waiting for Godot.

These lines parody existentialism and suggest that its exaggerated faith in man's rationality simply flatters his ego. As Esslin has noted, whereas Sartre's characters find themselves in an absurd world and act rationally, Beckett's characters find themselves in an absurd world and act absurdly.[16] In a similar vein Beckett contrasted his characters with those in Franz Kafka's novels: "The Kafka hero has a coherence of purpose. He's lost but he's not spiritually precarious, he's not falling to bits. My people seem to be falling to bits."[17]

For Sartre, Beckett's portrayal of man is pointless and even dangerous, since it does not incite us to action but instead suggests, as Estragon says in the opening line of *Godot,* that there is "nothing to be done."[18] Others may feel that there is a kind of optimism in Beckett's work, for despite the absurdity the characters go on. Whichever interpretation one prefers, it is clear that Beckett's representation of the absurdity of existence is extreme and in no way flatters man as existentialism does. His characters are among the most abject beings imaginable. The protagonists of *Waiting for Godot* are tramps with intellectual pretensions; in *Endgame* two characters are legless and lodged in trash cans; in *Play* the actors are encased in vases; in *Not I* (1972) we see nothing more than a mouth and a strange cloaked figure who listens to its ramblings; *That Time* (1976) puts on stage a bag-man, probably psychotic, who is prey to voices. In Beckett's trilogy the narrators fare no better: Molloy is a cripple who ends up in a ditch; Moran starts out as a good Irish burgher but finishes

19

as Molloy's double; Malone is a paralyzed internee of an institution who invents an alter ego named Saposcat (meaning "knower of excrement"); the Unnamable loses limbs progressively and ends up as a quadriplegic in a tray of sand or sawdust (not that he is deprived of all usefulness to society: he serves as a restaurant's signpost—complete with menu!). And in the novel *How It Is* wormlike creatures crawl through slime.

Physical fragmentation is accompanied by verbal disintegration, as we have already seen in Beckett's early work *Watt.* Molloy begins by writing normally, but soon his sentences grow longer and there are no new paragraphs after the second page. The stories Malone tells are constantly sabotaged before they end, and he is forced to stop mid-sentence as death approaches. The sentences toward the conclusion of *The Unnamable* are near-endless run-ons. Likewise, many of Beckett's theatrical characters speak nonstop. One of Beckett's most memorable scenes is Lucky's "think" in *Godot,* where for some three full pages a character spews forth fragments of philosophical discourse without interruption. In *Happy Days,* Winnie speaks often enough in grammatically correct sentences, but her gushing near-monologue lasts for over an hour. In *Play* and *Not I* speech is unpunctuated and almost constant. And if such monologue shows the disintegration of usual phrasing, then extremely rapid dialogue reduces conversation to mere automatism. Thus in *Waiting for Godot,* Estragon and Vladimir engage in quick repartee:

Vladimir:	Say you are, even it it's not true.
Estragon:	What am I to say?

Vladimir:	Say, I am happy.
Estragon:	I am happy.
Vladimir:	So am I.
Estragon:	So am I.
Vladimir:	We are happy.
Estragon:	We are happy. *(Silence.)* What do we do now, now that we are happy?
Vladimir:	Wait for Godot *(Estragon groans. Silence.)* (WFG 39)

Vladimir and Estragon appear to be having a conversation, but are merely echoing each other's words and linguistic rhythms. As critic Ruby Cohn noted in one of the first book-length studies on our author, Beckett consistently exploits to comic effect the reduction of the human to the mechanical.[19] So far does Beckett push linguistic disintegration that his works have become ever shorter since 1961—five or six pages is often enough to contain a late Beckett story or play. The shortest is the theater piece *Breath* (1969), where the curtain rises on an empty stage littered with rubbish. We hear an amplified breathing-in, a baby's cry, an amplified breathing-out, and the curtain falls.

Beckett has called *Breath* a "dramatic comma," as befits this punctuation mark that allows for breathing space.[20] We read in *The Unnamable:* "The comma will come where I'll drown for good, then the silence" (TN 409). Beckett uses other punctuation devices to give breathers: ellipses in *Not I:* "stare at her uncomprehending ... and now this stream ... steady stream ...

21

she who had never ... on the contrary ... practically speechless ..." (CSP 219), and periods in the latest works, such as *Mal vu mal dit* (1981, *Ill Seen Ill Said*): "Void. Nothing else. Contemplate that. Not another word. Home at last. Gently gently" (ISIS 31). *How It Is* dispenses with punctuation altogether, as blocks of texts alternate with blank spaces. The result is that the narrator is often left panting. Here he seems to be mispronouncing the word *mamma:*

> aha signifying mamma or some other thing some other sound barely audible signifying some other thing no matter the first to come and restore me to my dignity
>
> passing time is told to me and time past vast tracts of time the panting stops (H 26–27)

The *m* in *mamma* is a "fundamental sound," the first a baby utters, and one that serves to name several of Beckett's characters: Murphy, Mercier, Molloy, Mag, Moran, Malone, Macmann, Mahood, Maddy, Sam, Hamm, Pim, Bem, Bom, May, Amy. The narrator of *How It Is* speaks of his "thirst for labials" (H 108), that is, for labial consonants, consonants formed with the lips, like an *m* or *b*. As an object of thirst the *m* functions not simply as a unit of linguistic meaning but as a substance reminiscent of mother's milk.

The inverted form of the *m*, the *w*, begins other Beckett characters' names: Watt, Willie, Winnie, Worm. Indeed, "Worm" can be split up into the words *w or m*, suggesting a relationship between these two letters. To pronounce an *m* we must constrict the flow of air through our lips; to sound a *w* we must expel air through

22

the mouth. Thus *m* recalls the drinking of milk, whereas the *w* stands for the cry sounded to get the milk; more generally it is an emblem for the breath that plays such an important role in Beckett's works.

The materiality of Beckett's words has a counterpart in the physicality of his theater. Sartre's plays are often faulted on technical grounds: he had very little insight into the concrete exigencies of theater and was more interested in the text of the plays than their performance. Not so Beckett: the timing of the words and the gestures that accompany them are as essential as the words themselves. As Beckett said to his actress Billie Whitelaw while staging the play *Footfalls* (1976): "The words are only the excipient [i.e., the sugar on the pill]; the pacing is far more important."[21] Indeed, Beckett has even written pantomimes, explicitly called *Acts Without Words* (1957, 1960).

Most playwrights do not furnish stage directions for their plays; the instructions we read in the scripts were generally devised by the director for the first production. But Beckett includes very specific directions, and has often expressed displeasure when his works have been staged otherwise than as he planned. In according such importance to production Beckett aligns himself with the theories of Antonin Artaud. In *Le Théâtre et son double* (1938, translated as *The Theatre and Its Double*), Artaud claimed that Western theater was suffering under the tyranny of the text of the play, and that what was truly theatrical was production. Therefore he looked toward Asian theater, with its emphasis on ritualized body movement, dance, and music. Likewise, given the near bareness of the stage and the plot in most Beckett plays, the slightest gestures come to assume a ritual quality, even when that ritual is undermined by parody. Thus in *Godot,* Vladimir and Estragon perform an old vaudeville routine with three hats they pass back and forth; in *Endgame,* Clov scurries up and down a ladder he carries around the stage; in *Krapp's Last Tape,* Krapp chomps on bananas and throws the skins away while he paces to and fro.

In Beckett's later, shorter plays the actions are even simpler and more inexplicable; they can no longer be interpreted as symptoms of the characters' nervousness. In *Not I* the onstage listener to Mouth's monologue slowly spreads his arms in gestures of compassion that lessen in scope each time they occur; in *Footfalls* a character paces to and fro while speaking at an excruciatingly slow rate; in *Ohio Impromptu* (1981) the listener knocks repeatedly on the desk to interrupt the reader's words. None of these actions is terribly unusual; it is simply a question of how they are timed and executed. Completing Beckett's phrase, we may say that his work is not only a matter of fundamental sounds but also of fundamental actions.

The playwright whose *Waiting for Godot* and *Endgame* reflected the most important philosophical problem of this century—our awareness of our own absurdity—thus ends his career with short works structured around variations of gesture and voice. This shift from major to minor seems surprising, until we consider that his earlier masterpieces have helped us to come to terms with our absurdity. To continue to portray it in monumental form would now seem grandiose. Beckett's later, slight works correspond better to the little meaning he has taught us to expect from life.

NOTES

1. Martin Esslin, *The Theatre of the Absurd* (Woodstock, NY: Overlook Press, 1973) 19.

2. See, e.g., John Fletcher, "The Debt to Dante," *Samuel Beckett's Art* (London: Chatto and Windus, 1967) 106–21.

3. *Anthology of Mexican Poetry,* comp. by Octavio Paz (Bloomington: Indiana University Press, 1958).

4. Elmar Tophoven, personal communication.

5. Sartre, "Orphée noir," *Anthologie de la nouvelle poésie nègre et malgache de langue française,* ed. L. S. Senghor (Paris: Presses Universitares de France, 1948) xviii.

6. "Beckett's Letters on *Endgame,*" *Village Voice* 19 Mar. 1958: 15.

7. Quoted Ruby Cohn, *Back to Beckett* (Princeton: Princeton University Press, 1973) 58.

8. Quoted Cohn 58–59.

9. Personal interview with Beckett, 23 June 1983.

10. Jean-Michel Rey, "Sur Samuel Beckett," *Café Librairie* 1 (1983): 63, 64.

11. Freud, *Beyond the Pleasure Principle, Standard Edition* 18: 35

12. Walter Benjamin, "The Task of the Translator," *Illuminations,* trans. Harry Zohn (New York: Schocken, 1969) 69–82.

13. "Beckett's Letters on *Endgame*" 8.

14. Jacques Lacan, *Ecrits* (Paris: Editions du Seuil, 1966) 493, 495.

15. Sartre, *Being and Nothingness,* trans. Hazel E. Barnes (New York: Philosophical Library, 1956) 439.

16. Esslin 6.

17. Israel Shenker, "An Interview with Beckett (1956)," *Samuel Beckett: The Critical Heritage,* ed. Lawrence Graver and Raymond Federman (London: Routledge and Kegan Paul, 1979) 148

18. *Sartre on Theater,* ed. Michel Contat and Michel Rybalka, trans. Frank Jellinek (New York: Pantheon, 1976) 51, 99–100, 128.

19. Ruby Cohn, *Samuel Beckett: The Comic Gamut* (New Brunswick, NJ: Rutgers University Press, 1962) 288.

20. Raymond Federman, "Chronologie," Samuel Beckett, ed. Bishop and Federman (Paris: Editions de l'Herne, 1976) 350; my translation.

21. Beryl S. Fletcher and John Fletcher, *A Student's Guide to the Plays of Samuel Beckett* (London: Faber and Faber, 1985) 225.

CHAPTER TWO

Early Writings (1929–45)

In the overview we have seen how Beckett needed the excursus through a foreign language to achieve a "less-ness" in his writings. If his mature works are marked by a productive impoverishment, this suggests that the early ones are faulted by an excess of riches. But if there are riches, then it pays to enjoy them, even if their overabundance may suffocate us at times, as it did Beckett himself.

Beckett's best-known early works are essays on the authors James Joyce and Marcel Proust, a collection of short stories entitled *More Pricks than Kicks,* the novels *Murphy* and *Watt,* and several short poems. The first critical piece, entitled "Dante ... Bruno . Vico. . Joyce" (so punctuated because the periods are meant to represent the number of centuries between the various authors), had its origin in Beckett's friendship in Paris with Joyce, another Irishman seeking refuge from his native land's provincialism. When Beckett met him in 1928, Joyce had already achieved notoriety as the author of the short stories in *Dubliners* (1914), the semi-autobiographical *A Portrait of the Artist as a Young Man* (1916), and the censored *Ulysses* (1922). The last work begins as a continuation of *Portrait* but soon abandons any ordinary organization as it reproduces more and more its characters' "stream of consciousness."

During the period Beckett knew him Joyce was

completing an even more radical literary experiment than *Ulysses:* the so-called *Work in Progress,* which in final form would be published as *Finnegans Wake* (1939). If *Ulysses* used the technique of stream of consciousness, this last work of Joyce's brings to bear the flow of the unconscious as it can be heard in the puns and "Freudian slips" that reveal to the patient in analysis the thoughts of which he himself was unaware.

Each word in *Finnegans Wake* functions as any other that sounds like it; an example is the title, which resonates as "Finnegan's wake" (that is, Finnegan's funeral), "Finnegan's awake" (that is, he's not sleeping), "Finnegans wake" (an imperative addressed to the Finnegan family to awaken, or a declarative that says they stay awake), just to mention a few possibilities. The effect is even more dizzying when we consider that Joyce incorporated elements from some seventy languages. Thus when one character is described as being "yung and easily freudened"—an allusion to the childhood traumas that so preoccupied Freud and his Swiss disciple Carl Jung—we do not only read the names of two psychoanalysts and a deformation of the English expression "young and easily frightened." We also hear the German words *jung,* meaning "young," and *Freude,* meaning "joy"—but here *Freude* is forced to signify something contrary to joy: fright! This *freudened,* combining *Freud, Freude,* and *frightened,* functions as a portmanteau word like *motel,* meaning *mot*or ho*tel.* Such multilingual portmanteaus can be found on every page of *Finnegans Wake.*

To complicate matters further, Joyce's work does not proceed as a linear narrative. Basing himself on the cyclical historical theories of the Italian Enlightenment thinker Giambattista Vico, he presents in *Finne-gans Wake* an allegory of universal history in circular form. The first sentence, "riverrun, past Eve and Adam's, from swerve of shore to bend of bay, brings us by a commodius vicus of recirculation back to Howth Castle and Environs," appears to be a fragment but is actually the completion of the book's last sentence: "A way a lone a last a loved a long the." Thus the book is entirely round, with no beginning or end.

One can understand how with a style so allusive—and elusive—Joyce was afraid lest his work not be appreciated. He requested several of his intimates to write exegeses of it, to be collected in a volume with the Joycean title *Our Exagmination Round his Factification for Incamination of Work in Progress* (1929). *Factification* would no doubt mean "putting into effect" or "making into fact"; *incamination* could well mean "getting under way" (*camin* is a Latin root for "road"); and the *g* in "exagmination" adds a whimsical but also disfiguring touch to the word. Thus Beckett's Molloy shows how his mother's name is changed through the addition of a *g:* "I called her Mag because for me, without knowing why, the letter g abolished the syllable Ma, and as it were spat on it, better than any other letter would have done" (TN 17).

Like the *g* that abolishes the syllable "Ma," so Beckett's "exagmination" of the *Work in Progress* points to its ultimate unexaminability: *Finnegans Wake* falls into no preexisting categories. Thus Beckett, writing on the influence of Italian thinkers on Joyce, warns us that "the danger is in the neatness of identifications" (D 19). For example, Dante is usually thought of as the first author to write high poetry in the commonly spoken language rather than Latin, yet Beckett shows us what is simplistic about that viewpoint:

> [Dante] did not write in Florentine any more than in Neapolitan. He wrote a vulgar that *could* have been spoken by an ideal Italian who had assimilated what was best in all the dialects of his own country, but which in fact was certainly not spoken nor ever had been (D 30).

Hence the parallel Beckett draws between Dante and Joyce. Dante created a new Italian language by amalgamating several dialects, and Joyce forged a new language by fusing elements of seventy tongues. The languages in which Dante and Joyce write are not natural but invented by them—just as we saw (in chapter 1 above) that Beckett comes to create something of his own language, in both English and French.

Moreover, Beckett reminds us in his essay on Joyce that all language is invented:

> "The animals were given names by Adam," the man who "first said goo to a goose." Moreover it is explicitly stated that the choice of names was left entirely to Adam, so that there is not the slightest Biblical authority for the conception of language as a direct gift of God (D 31).

In the phrase Beckett quotes from *Finnegans Wake,* "first said goo to a goose," we hear the kind of "fundamental sound" that Beckett will say his own work consists of; and as such sounds demand that Beckett's words be read aloud, so Beckett wrote that *Finnegans Wake* "is not only to be read. It is to be looked at and listened to" (D 27). We have also seen how in Beckett's work content repeats form, when the characters repeatedly say that they repeat themselves and reproduce the silence of which they speak in the pauses between their words. Likewise, Beckett says of Joyce's *Work in Progress:* "Here form *is* content, content *is* form. [...] His writing is not *about* something; *it is that something itself*" (D 27). In *Molloy,* Beckett will also make language coincide with what it speaks of, posing an equivalence between "doing" and "saying": "whatever I do, that is to say whatever I say" (TN 45); and in *L'Innommable* (98), he will write, "Ce qui se passe, ce sont des mots." Beckett deleted from the English *Unnamable* this sentence, which means: *Words are what is happening.*

Beckett addresses the same question in the monograph entitled *Proust* (1931), which he devoted to Marcel Proust's voluminous semiautobiographical opus, *A la recherche du temps perdu* (1913–27, translated as *Remembrance of Things Past*). Like Joyce, Proust "makes no attempt to dissociate form from content" (P 67). The indissoluble marriage of the two emerges in the Proustian experience of involuntary memory. In the most famous scene from the *Recherche,* the narrator dips a teacake into a cup of herbal tea. On biting into it, he is reminded of a similar taste sensation in childhood, and suddenly all his memories of summering in the village of Combray come forth from this cup of tea. The purely formal repetition of the act takes on the emotional and intellectual content of its original occurrence. Beckett tells us that in such moments of involuntary memory the Proustian hero experiences "the total past sensation, not its echo nor its copy, but the sensation itself, annihilating every spatial and temporal restriction" (P 54).

Thus the memory reexperienced in its plenitude does not simply symbolize something that occurred before; rather, "it is that something itself," to use the formula Beckett employed with respect to Joyce. "For Proust the object may be a living symbol, but a symbol of itself" (P 60). A symbol usually evokes something other than itself, so if it refers back to itself, symbolic meaning has been troubled. This too foreshadows Beckett's later writing. To take the most famous example: it seems clear that in *Waiting for Godot,* Godot symbolizes something. Is he God (as the name Godot suggests), or the simple necessity to go on? Or, rather, is he the symbol of the impossibility of assigning a stable symbolic meaning? When asked what Godot stands for, Beckett replied that if he knew, he would have said so in the play.[1] According to Beckett himself, at least, his writings symbolize little beyond themselves.

Hence Beckett was not criticizing when he wrote that Proust's object is a "symbol of itself." If for Proust the object appears the same in the initial experience as in its remembrance, it is divorced from the accidents of time and emerges in its essence. In this way involuntary memory reveals being. Insofar as the nature of being is one of the main concerns of philosophy, French critic Bernard Brun has suggested that Beckett was well before his time in placing a philosophical question at the heart of his study of Proust.[2] For until recently most works on Proust dealt with him from a literary rather than a philosophical perspective.

Beckett says that Proust's revelation of being through involuntary memory is a kind of *Discourse on Method,* a reference to the work by the seventeenth-century French philosopher René Descartes. The comparison

31

of Proust to Descartes is partially ironic, for what kind of method can there be in the purely accidental discoveries attributable to involuntary memory? Rather, Proust stands at the antipodes of Descartes, the philosopher best remembered for his philosophy of systematic doubt. Putting everything into question, he finds that the only thing he cannot doubt is that he is thinking. Hence the famous expression *cogito ergo sum*—"I think, therefore I am"—the point of departure from which he makes his entire system proceed in linear fashion. In this way Descartes claims he imitates

> travelers who, finding themselves lost in a forest, ought not wander round, going this way and that . . . but ought always walk as straight a line as they can in one direction, . . . for by this means, if they are not going where they wish, they will finally arrive at least somewhere where they probably will be better off than in the middle of a forest.[3]

It was during Beckett's first stay in Paris that he read philosophy most intensely; thus he frequented Descartes, Proust, and Joyce simultaneously. We have seen how Proust and Descartes make for strange company; the same is true of Descartes and Joyce. Descartes, the philosopher who places his faith in conscious thought and linear, organized progression, stands in opposition to Joyce, who plays upon the unconscious and makes his work proceed in a circle. Beckett ultimately harmonizes these two opposites, as can be seen in these lines from *Molloy,* which rewrite in ironic fashion the above passage from Descartes:

> having heard, or more probably read somewhere [. . .] that when a man in a forest thinks he is going for-

ward in a straight line, in reality he is going in a circle, I did my best to go in a circle, hoping in this way to go in a straight line (TN 85).

It will take Beckett years to achieve this synthesis between Joyce and Descartes. Instead, his first attempt to join the two led to the obfuscation of Descartes by Joyce. Beckett's early poem "Whoroscope" (1930), which plays upon details of Descartes's life, is through and through a Joycean creation. The title is a portmanteau word, merging "who," "whore," and "horoscope." The question "who?" is appropriate, for the poem is so hermetic that Beckett supplies notes at its end to aid in its comprehension. It is only there that we find out that the poem is about Descartes at all, and that he did not want his horoscope cast. Likewise, the beginning of the poem:

> What's that?
> An egg?
> By the brothers Boot it stinks fresh.
> Give it to Gillot (CP 1)

can only be elucidated through Beckett's notes to the effect that Descartes could not abide omelets made from recently laid eggs, that "in 1640 the brothers Boot refuted Aristotle in Dublin," and that "Descartes passed on the easier problems in analytic geometry to his valet Gillot" (CP 5).

Beckett's Joycean mode continues into his first book of fiction, *More Pricks than Kicks,* a collection of stories loosely tied together into a novel. Like "Whoroscope" the title is prurient and allusive. In this case the reference is to a verse from Acts (9:5); when Saul of Tarsus feels guilt about persecuting Christians because he is beginning to believe in Jesus himself, he is told not "to kick against the pricks," that is, not to resist his pangs of conscience but instead accept Christ. More important than the scriptural reference is the resonance of the words. "Pricks" obviously suggests penises, but insofar as it stands in opposition to "kicks," which means fun, *More Pricks than Kicks* can be read as "more pain than fun." This title describes well the lot of the protagonist, Belacqua Shuah, who suffers various sexual misfortunes. Two of his wives die shortly after he weds them (he implored one of them to take a lover, so he could obtain a voyeuristic thrill while avoiding intercourse), and he dies shortly after a third marriage.

Belacqua Shuah's name carries the mark of his frustration. Shuah is the maternal grandfather of the ill-fated Onan in Genesis (38:8–10), punished for engaging in coitus interruptus. It is interesting that Shuah is in Onan's maternal lineage, for the final *a* of Belacqua suggests a female character. Though the original Belacqua, a character from Dante (*Purgatorio,* canto 4), was a man, he was feminized in his passivity. A Florentine lute maker condemned to Purgatory, Belacqua had to remain seated, head drooping between his legs, because during his life he had been dilatory about seeking salvation. This image of immobility pleased Beckett, for Belacqua is mentioned in *Murphy, Molloy, How It Is,* and *The Lost Ones;* elsewhere one finds characters resting in the Belacqua position.

Belacqua Shuah is a strange name for an Irishman, but Belacqua is an unusual Irishman. Like his creator, whose initials he shares, Belacqua is a "dirty low-church Protestant" in a nation of Catholics, and he enjoys foreign languages, "setting aside a portion of each day for polyglot splendours" (MPTK 73, 129). The book opens on Belacqua deciphering a difficult passage from Dante, where the beloved Beatrice explains to the poet the spots on the moon. The relationship between Dante and Beatrice is parodied in the one between Belacqua and his middle-aged Italian instructress. When Belacqua asks her to translate a pun from Dante, she first remains silent, then finally murmurs: "Do you think […] it is absolutely necessary to translate it?" Belacqua's multilingual frolic is cut short, and he feels "like a fool" (MPTK 19). It is as though there were a guilt associated with the desire to translate.

A bad conscience over the study of languages was already portrayed by Joyce in "The Dead," the final story in *Dubliners*. There the protagonist who wants to practice languages other than Gaelic is taken to task by an Irish nationalist, as castrating a woman as Belacqua's Italian teacher. The scene from Beckett can be read as an ironic rewriting of the Joyce passage, for whereas Joyce's work involves the important issues of Irish nationalism, the concerns of Beckett's character seem trivially erudite. Moreover, in *Dubliners* Joyce portrays with great compassion those caught up in the impasses of Ireland's provincial capital, while Beckett parodies his Dubliners in *More Pricks than Kicks*. Thus we read in the beginning of the chapter entitled "Love and Lethe": "The Toughs, consisting of Mr and Mrs and their one and only Ruby, lived in a small house in Irishtown" (MPTK 85).

This mock-storybook beginning points to another element of *More Pricks than Kicks:* the emphasis on the factitiousness of the narrative. We are often reminded that the story and characters are not real and

35

that we are reading a literary work. For example, in reintroducing a character Beckett refers explicitly to an earlier story in the volume: "Alba Perdue, it may be remembered, was the nice little girl in *A Wet Night*" (MPTK 127). In other cases footnotes recall by name a previous chapter where an event under consideration occurred. Emphasis on the fictional nature of the narrative begins with its first sentence: "It was morning and Belacqua was stuck in the first of the canti in the moon." The "canti in the moon" are chapters in Dante's *Paradiso;* thus Belacqua is "stuck" on a literary planet rather than on our real one. Moreover, the improbabilities of the plot (such as Belacqua's multiple marriages followed by his wives' demise or his own death), as well as the chronological gaps between the chapters, make us aware that we are following a fiction rather than a life.

The facticity of the narrative is foregrounded as well in Beckett's next novel, *Murphy.* The first sentence— "The sun shone, having no alternative, on the nothing new"—pretends to give us information about the real world; it claims to tell us that the novel's action takes place on a planet in all respects like ours, in which on a given day it can be sunny rather than rainy. However, this sentence actually places the narrative *within language itself,* within old and oft-repeated language, referring it to the saying from Ecclesiastes 1:9, "There is nothing new under the sun."

In *Murphy,* Beckett reminds us in other ways that we are reading a book. As in *More Pricks than Kicks* he refers explicitly to the book's division into chapters: in the first pages we are told that Murphy's mind will be "described in section six," that is, in the sixth chapter. Likewise, Beckett addresses the reader directly as "gentle skimmer" (M 84) and the typesetter as "gentle compositor" (M 236). He even makes reference to the Irish censor who he knows will condemn his book. Calling fornication "music," he comments that "this phrase is chosen with care, lest the filthy censors should lack an occasion to commit their filthy synecdoche" (M 76). A similar narrative strategy appears when we are told that "the above passage is carefully calculated to deprave the cultivated reader" (M 118). And the narrator repeatedly points to his reworking of the characters' words:

> Celia's account, expurgated, accelerated, improved and reduced, of how she came to have to speak of Murphy, gives the following (M 12).

> Neary's account, expurgated, accelerated, improved and reduced, of how he came to reach the end of Cork endurance, gives the following (M 48).

> Celia's confidence to Mr. Kelly, Neary's to Wylie, had to be given for the most part obliquely. With all the more reason now, Ticklepenny's to Murphy. It will not take many moments (M 87).

> Cooper's account, expurgated, accelerated, improved and reduced, of how he came to be turned off, gives the following (M 119).

One splendid passage wreaks havoc upon the tradition of character description. In *More Pricks than Kicks* the narrator remarks that "it would be a waste of time to itemise" Belacqua's first wife, Lucy (MPTK 105), but with regard to Murphy's Celia, such itemization is well worth it. For this is how she is presented to us:

Age.	Unimportant.
Head.	Small and round.
Eyes.	Green.
Complexion.	White.
Hair.	Yellow.
Features.	Mobile.
Neck.	13–3/4".
Upper arm.	11".
Forearm.	9–1/2".
Wrist.	6".
Bust.	34".
Waist.	27".
Hips, etc.	35".
Thigh.	21–3/4". (M 10)

Celia's portrait is exact, but it hardly works to give us a "realistic" view of her. Moreover, as in *More Pricks than Kicks,* a convoluted plot undoes any realism and makes the prose somewhat "nervous," to use the adjective that French critic Ludovic Janvier has applied to this book.[4]

Murphy is an Irishman come to London to seek a job in order to marry his fiancée, Miss Counihan. She in turn is being wooed in his absence by his former professor Neary as well as by Neary's student Wylie. In London, Murphy meets a prostitute, Celia, who replaces Miss Counihan in his affections, unbeknownst to Miss Counihan. Thus two men associated with Murphy are after Murphy's fiancée, and she and another woman are after Murphy. The unlikeliness of such a protagonist-centered universe is underscored by the narrator:

Everything led to Murphy (M 66).

Murphy then is actually being needed by five people outside himself (M 202).

All the puppets in this book whinge sooner or later, except Murphy, who is not a puppet (M 122).

In this last quotation we see a difference between *Murphy* and *More Pricks than Kicks*. Whereas in the earlier text the characters are unidimensional, in the later novel at least the protagonist has some substance. And the substance of which he is made is mind.

The sixth chapter of the novel, in which Murphy's mind is described, is a sublime parody of philosophical discourse. If philosophy is a search for the truth, be it the truth of being or of mind, section 6 presents Murphy's mind not "as it really was [...] but solely [as] it felt and pictured itself to be" (M 107). We are at two removes from philosophy proper: rather than having mind revealed, we are introduced to Murphy's mind—and not as it was, but as it conceived itself.

Believing his mind to be completely separate from his body, Murphy follows Descartes, who posited the mind-body dichotomy. Yet whereas Descartes held that the two are linked in the pineal gland or *conarium,* his student Geulincx—who is referred to in *Murphy* as well as *Molloy*—theorized that mind and body are nowhere connected. Our body executes what our mind sets out to do because God intervenes in each act of volition.

In chapter 1, Neary had remarked that Murphy's "conarium has shrunk to nothing" (M 6). Like a good Geulincxian, Murphy believes in the radical separation between mind and body:

He was satisfied that neither [mind nor body] followed from the other. He neither thought a kick because he felt one nor felt a kick because he thought one. [...] Perhaps there was, outside space and time, a non-mental, non-physical Kick from all eternity, dimly revealed to Murphy in its correlated modes of consciousness and extension, the kick *in intellectu* and the kick *in re* (M 109).

In this passage on the Platonic essence of a thing above and beyond all individual occurrences of it, philosophical jargon is ridiculed. The object of philosophy is no longer being or truth, but rather a kick—a word that in a Beckett work must remind use of the title *More Pricks than Kicks*.

Not only Plato and Descartes but the nineteenth-century German philosopher Hegel as well is parodied in *Murphy*. According to Hegel, mind works itself out through the tripartite movement of thesis, antithesis, and synthesis. A thesis is posited, then it is negated, and ultimately thesis and antithesis are reconciled in an *Aufhebung,* a word meaning both cancellation and conservation, and often translated as "sublation." In *Murphy* these stages of mind are made roundly physical:

Neary clenched his fists and raised them before his face. [...]

The knuckles stood out white under the skin in the usual way—this was the *position*. The hands then opened quite correctly to the utmost limit of their compass—that was the *negation*. It now seemed to Murphy that there were two equally legitimate ways in which the gesture might be concluded, and the *sublation* effected. The hands might be clapped to the head in a smart gesture of despair, or let fall limply to the seams of the trousers (M 4–5, emphasis added).

Philosophy is not the only science applied ironically in *Murphy*. The protagonist's request for a cup of tea and biscuits—reminiscent of Proust's famous tea-cake scene—is explained in terms of associationist psychology, with its coupling of stimulus and response:

"Bring me" [. . .]. He paused after this preparatory signal to let the fore-period develop, that first of the three moments of reaction in which, according to the Külpe school, the major torments of the *response* are undergone. Then he applied the *stimulus* proper. "A cup of tea and a packet of assorted biscuits" (M 80, emphasis added).

Likewise, Gestalt psychology with its theory of figure and ground is parodied when Neary's love affair with a Miss Dwyer is described as finished: "No sooner had Miss Dwyer [. . .] made Neary as happy as a man could desire, than she became one with the ground against which she had figured so prettily" (M 48). Psychoanalysis is parodied when "the little ego and the big id" are called "infinite riches in a w.c." (M 218)—the Freudian unconscious thereby reduced to a reservoir of dirty secrets. Likewise, the belief of some Jungians that one can remember not only one's birth but the event that caused it is ridiculed when Neary "curse[s], first the day in which he was born, then—in a bold flash-back— the night in which he was conceived" (M 46).

As befits this book so concerned with various psychologies Murphy ultimately lands a job as an attendant in an insane asylum. There he encounters "the race of people he had long since despaired of finding," those whose lives were "immured in mind, as he insisted on supposing" (M 169, 180). In this last sentence the narrator—who knows, as Lacan would say, that "one does not become mad because one wants to"[5]— sets himself above the character, who wishes to join the insane. Such a strategy recalls the mocking narrator in *More Pricks than Kicks;* yet whereas Belacqua never achieves the superior knowledge possessed by the narrator, Murphy does come to understand that the universe inhabited by schizophrenics is not the self-conscious pure mind of philosophy.[6] By looking into the blank stare of the psychotic Mr. Endon, Murphy sees that the patient is truly conscious of nothing. Realizing that he "is a speck in Mr. Endon's unseen" (M 250), Murphy soon ends up as specks of matter. He dies in a conflagration caused by gas escaping from a leak, and his ashes, dropped on a barroom floor, are swept away with the sawdust.

In *Murphy* the protagonist was not mad himself, but only fascinated with the mad. Beckett's next novel, *Watt,* the last he wrote in English, portrays a character who himself bears many of the earmarks of schizophrenia. Freud writes in his article entitled "The Unconscious" that rather than being simply an illness, schizophrenia shows the attempt of the patient to regain health.[7] Having made a break with the world, the schizophrenic tries to reestablish contact with it and make sense of it by investing psychic energy in the words that stand for the objects he left behind. Likewise, Beckett's *Watt* attempts to reconstruct his world on the basis of words.

In approaching *Watt* the reader has to do some reconstruction of his own, for the book uses a disjointed style, which at times suggests the speech of psychotics. The difficulty of the book has little to do with the events recounted, in themselves quite ordinary. In part 1 Watt arrives at a streetcar stop and directs himself to the home of Mr. Knott, whose servant he is to become. Part 2 recounts Watt's domestic routine and musings during the year he spent as a servant on the ground floor. Part 3 tells us the same about Watt's year as a servant on the upper floor. Unlike the other parts, it is narrated in the first person, by a friend of Watt's named Sam, who seems to have been a fellow inmate at a mental institution. Part 4 returns to the anonymous third-person narration to tell of Watt's departure.

We note here the extreme reduction of plot, foreshadowing Beckett's later works, in which the movement of language takes on greater importance than the characters' stories. This tendency is clear from the very beginning of *Watt:*

Mr. Hackett turned the corner and saw, in the failing light, at some little distance, his seat. It seemed to be occupied. This seat, the property very likely of the municipality, or of the public, was of course not his, but he thought of it as his. This was Mr. Hack-

43

ett's attitude towards things that pleased him. He knew they were not his, but he thought of them as his. He knew they were not his, because they pleased him (w 7).

Here we already detect the rhythm that will become typical in Beckett: the alternation between sound and silence, brought about by the commas between the words. The first sentence is legato ("in the failing light, at some little distance"), whereas the last two have parallel staccato rhythms ("He knew they were not his, but he thought of them as his. He knew they were not his, because they pleased him"). It is interesting, moreover, that Mr. Hackett is aware that the seat he thinks of as his own belongs not to him but to the public; this play on ownership foreshadows the relationship to language in *The Unnamable,* where the narrator feels that he is speaking a tongue that is not his own, and that he only has the words of others.

The beginning of *Watt,* which speaks of where Mr. Hackett will sit, symbolizes the trouble we readers have in *sit*uating what occurs in this novel. It also exemplifies the difficulty. How can a novel "begin" by stating that a "Mr. Hackett *turned the corner*"? Turning a corner implies that one was on another road before, a road here not mentioned. Although such a beginning in midstream has a literary pedigree in the tradition of *in medias res,* it is no true beginning at all. We are already lost at the start of the text.

Beckett, too, gets displaced, for his name is deformed into Hackett (suggesting hack writer), and Mr. Hackett is only a secondary character. No better fate is reserved for the other Beckett namesake, the narrator of part 3 called Sam, a former internee at a mental institution. The author's self-parody here symbolizes the instability he brings to the narrative. For this is the first book by Beckett that makes us wonder, time and again, who is speaking.

It is true that in *More Pricks than Kicks,* Beckett had already varied narrative voice: the chapter "Ding-Dong" is recounted by a friend of Belacqua's, and "The Smeraldina's Billet Doux" takes the form of a letter from a female admirer of Belacqua. Yet these texts are exceptions; in that novel, as in *Murphy,* the narrator is an omniscient one, who on occasion is smug toward the characters. In *Watt* such distance between the narrator and characters is all but effaced, as is shown by the absence of quotation marks around words they utter. This technique, which Joyce had already used, makes it impossible to differentiate between the characters' speech and the narrator's. The effect is clear when Mr. Hackett attempts to denounce to a policeman a couple he believes is committing an obscene act:

> Officer, he cried, as God is my witness, he had his hand upon it.
> God is a witness that cannot be sworn.
> If I interrupted your beat, said Mr. Hackett, a thousand pardons (w 9).

The words "God is a witness that cannot be sworn" cannot with certainty be imputed either to the policeman or to the narrator. This indeterminacy becomes more important in the long monologues that make up much of this book. For example, pages 39 to 63 consist of a discourse by Arsene, Watt's predecessor in Mr. Knott's household. Perhaps it is even misleading to

45

speak of a distinction between the narrator's and characters' voices, for the suddenness with which the monologues are introduced and ended, their sheer length, and the lack of quotation marks around them make them narrative voices as well. Thus we experience an interweaving of different voices, an emblem for which is provided by the two scores for mixed choir (human and frog) included in the book. Insofar as modulation of voices comes to play a role in *Watt,* it is the first important work of Beckett's to leave behind the purely novelistic and assume a theatrical quality.

In our discussion we have lost sight of Watt—or actually we have not yet seen him. For Watt does not show up until several pages into the book; and when he does appear, the question of perspective is raised again. We see him from the viewpoint of Mr. Hackett and Goff and Tetty Nixon, a couple at the tram stop with whom Mr. Hackett was speaking:

> Tetty was not sure whether it was a man or a woman. Mr. Hackett was not sure that it was not a parcel, a carpet for example, or a roll of tarpaulin, wrapped up in a dark paper and tied about the middle with a cord (w 16).

Thus the question Watt represents for the Nixons and Mr. Hackett is the one his name suggests, for Watt resonates as "what." Moreover, this is the question that Watt addresses to the world time and again, and the answers he receives do not always satisfy him. This is evident in the passage quoted in chapter 1 above, where Watt fails in his attempts to make the word *pot* adhere to the object it names, and succeeds only in making the word rhyme with Watt and Knott. These names suggest that the question *what?* is *knotty,* that the answer may *not* exist at all, and that the whole text might be just a lot of *what-not*—just so much rigmarole.[8] The entire book might be no more than plays with language.

Beckett has never claimed that he writes more than that: remember his comment to the effect that his work is "a matter of fundamental sounds." Thus Beckett puts to good use the schizophrenic experience of the separation between word and thing, but there is a difference between his superior attitude toward words isolated from objects and that of his character. Watt, not content with such separation, attempts to forge links between word and thing. We see this when he is told to give the remains of Mr. Knott's dinner "to the dog" (w 91). Now the expression "leave something for the dog" functions as linguistic reflex; one may say "leave it for *the* dog" even when one owns no dog, for one presumes that a dog or some other animal will come by to eat food left on a doorstep. Leaving it for "the" dog really means leaving it for "a" dog.

Yet Watt does not understand the words in that way, and so imagines—for several pages on end—a family named Lynch, paid by Mr. Knott to care for a dog always hungry enough to eat leftovers: "Five generations, twenty-eight souls, nine hundred and eighty years, such was the proud record of the Lynch family" (w 103–04).

One could say that Watt's imagination is running away with him, but this creation of a whole lineage on the basis of the expression "leave it for the dog" is typical of the process whereby this book generates narrative through literalism. Thus Arthur, Watt's successor as ground-floor servant to Mr. Knott, tells of his friend whose university examiners "looked at one another":

> when five men look at one another, though in theory only twenty looks are necessary, every man looking four times, yet in practice this number is seldom sufficient, on account of the multitude of looks that go astray. For example, Mr. Fitzwein looked at Mr. Magershon, on his right. But Mr. Magershon is not looking at Mr. Fitzwein, on his left, but at Mr. O'Meldon, on his right. But Mr. O'Meldon is not looking at Mr. Magershon, on his left, but, craning forward, at Mr. MacStern (w 175).

This passage goes on for five pages. It shows the functioning of another mechanism for textual production: the permutation. This strategy is often exploited in this novel, as when we hear of the voices Mr. Watt hears:

> Now these voices, sometimes they sang only, and sometimes they cried only, and sometimes they stated only, and sometimes they murmured only, and sometimes they sang and cried, and sometimes they sang and stated, and sometimes they sang and murmured, and sometimes they cried and stated, and sometimes they cried and murmured, and sometimes they stated and murmured (w 29).

There is a series of verbs—"sang," "cried," "stated," and "murmured"—and the sentence is constructed by recombining them in an organized manner: first, each verb is used alone; then the first verb is paired with the second, third, and fourth; and then the second verb is paired with the third and fourth; and then the third is paired with the fourth. In mathematical notation the couples are: 1,2; 1,3; 1,4; 2,3; 2,4; 3,4. If we felt before that Watt's imagination was running away with him, here we feel that language itself is going amok. It is as though the words were recombining themselves in the absence of any consciousness, according to mechanical rules. Thus we understand what Beckett meant when he said that in writing *Watt* language was "running away" with him.[9] It is at this point in his career that he switched to French, feeling that a foreign language would force him to use words more carefully.

NOTES

1. Quoted by Alan Schneider, "Waiting for Beckett: A Personal Chronicle," *Casebook on* Waiting for Godot, ed. Ruby Cohn (New York: Grove, 1967) 55.

2. Bernard Brun, "Sur le *Proust* de Beckett," *Beckett avant Beckett,* ed. Jean-Michel Rabaté (Paris: Presses de l'Ecole Normale Supérieure, 1984) 80.

3. Descartes, *Discourse on Method and Meditations on First Philosophy,* trans. Donald A. Cress (Indianapolis: Hackett, 1980) 13. I have modified the translation somewhat to conform more closely to the original.

4. Ludovic Janvier, *Pour Samuel Beckett* (Paris: Editions de Minuit, 1966) 25.

5. Jacques Lacan, *Ecrits* (Paris: Editions du Seuil, 1966) 176; my translation.

6. This reading of madness in *Murphy* owes much to Rabaté's "Quelques figures de la première (et dernière) anthropomorphie de Beckett," Rabaté 135–51.

7. Freud, "The Unconscious," *Standard Edition* 14:203–04.

8. Ruby Cohn, "Watt Knott," *Samuel Beckett: The Comic Gamut* (New Brunswick, NJ: Rutgers University Press, 1962) 65–94.

9. Personal interview with Beckett, 23 June 1983.

CHAPTER THREE

Major Novels (1947–61)

Beckett's first prose work to be published in French was written shortly after the war. This was the story "Suite" ("Continuation"), which appeared in truncated form in the July 1946 issue of Sartre's journal, *Les Temps Modernes*. Beckett would later publish the piece in its entirety as "La Fin" ("The End"), along with several other short pieces, in *Nouvelles et Textes pour rien* (1955, translated as *Stories and Texts for Nothing*). Many of the themes and situations evoked in that volume are developed more fully in the better-known trilogy Beckett wrote in French between 1947 and 1949, made up of the novels *Molloy* (later translated into English under the same title), *Malone meurt (Malone Dies)*, and *L'Innommable (The Unnamable)*.

Molloy

On the back of the most recent French paperback edition of *Molloy* is this quotation from one of the first reviews of the work: "If one can speak of an event in literature, this book is uncontestably an event".[1]

At first sight this "literary event" seems unassuming. It starts with a rather ordinary sentence: "Je suis dans la chambre de ma mère," translated by Beckett in collaboration with South African poet Patrick Bowles as "I am in my mother's room." But the sentence is already literary, insofar as it harks back to the beginning of Albert Camus's *L'Etranger* (1942, *The Stranger*): "Mother died today. Or, maybe, yesterday." Beckett's writing in *Molloy* resembles Camus's in certain ways. They are both prime examples of what the French call *écriture blanche,* white, blank, neutral writing, devoid of usual literary embellishments. But Beckett parts company with Camus as he did with Sartre. *The Stranger* presents absurd events—the narrator's gratuitous murder of a man and the ensuing trial, which does not address the charges—in a well-ordered manner, whereas *Molloy* tells us absurd stories in an absurd way.

There is, however, one formally troubling element in *The Stranger:* we never learn how the jailed narrator managed to write or dictate his story. It is as though the account sprang fully formed from the teller's head, but nowhere is this absurdity addressed. In *Molloy,* on the contrary, we are offered an explanation for how the narrative came into existence; the only problem is that it seems to presuppose an impossible chronology. We learn in the first paragraph that Molloy, the narrator of the first half of the book, sits in a room and writes pages that are collected by a man who

> told me I'd begun all wrong, that I should have begun differently. He must be right. I began at the beginning, like an old ballocks, can you imagine that? Here's my beginning. Because they're keeping it apparently (TN 8).

If this is the beginning as it stood when he first wrote the text, then how could he incorporate into this "original beginning" the objections made to it? Upon a second reading we realize that this is prefatory material, that the word "beginning" refers to the start of the account in the second paragraph. But Beckett has already undermined our confidence that we can understand this text in a direct manner.

Our unsure comprehension is all the more unsettling as Molloy's narrative flows smoothly. So smoothly, in fact, that after the first paragraph of 500 words, the second part of his monologue consists of a paragraph of 40,000 words. As in *Watt,* language seems to be running away from the narrator, but there is a difference. In *Watt* the omniscient narrator never admitted he was out of control, but in *Molloy* that feeling is voiced time and again. On the first page, we read:

> I don't know how to work any more. [...] The truth is I haven't much will left. [...] The truth is I don't know much. [...] It's impossible that I could ever have helped anyone. I've forgotten how to spell too, and half the words.

Later on, we learn from an offhand comment that our writer cannot even read: "I had read with care, while I still could read, accounts of travellers" (TN 31). The logical constraint of noncontradiction does not hold in this world.

Molloy's mental impotence has a physical counterpart, for he is first crippled in one leg and then in both. Considering such a state, Moran—the narrator of the second half of *Molloy*—addresses a paean to bodily impotence:

> To be literally incapable of motion at last, that must be something! My mind swoons when I think of it. And mute into the bargain! And perhaps as deaf as

a post! And who knows as blind as a bat! And as likely as not your memory a blank! And just enough brain intact to allow you to exult (TN 140).

Moran's glorification of paralysis corresponds to Beckett's praise of impotence: remember that he chose to write in French because it allowed him to assume his weakness in the face of language. In this way he is like Molloy, who asks, "Where did I get this access of vigour? From my weakness perhaps" (TN 84).

Beckett did not rid himself of the runaway language he experienced in *Watt;* instead, he learned to exploit its uncontrollability as a way to write. Thus Molloy's description of his journey to find his mother can be likened to Beckett's writing:

I went on my way, that way of which I knew nothing, qua way, which was nothing more than a surface, bright or dark, smooth or rough, and always dear to me, in spite of all, and the dear sound of that which goes and is gone, with a brief dust, when the weather is dry. There I am then, before I knew I had left the town, on the canal-bank (TN 26).

The first sentence begins sensibly enough, but as Molloy starts describing his ignorance of his own path, the sentence wanders off into a completely unexpected area, suddenly speaking of sound. Then Molloy moves back to his journey, only to mention his surprise at finding himself at a place where he has arrived he knows not how.

If it is difficult for Molloy to follow his own movements, it is no easier for us. Therefore, as we recapitulate some of the salient points of his narrative, we must bear in mind that such linear construction of a plot does violence to a text that follows the narrator's ruminations in all directions.

Molloy is a vagabond, a hobo. We find him at the beginning stationary in his mother's room, but that is not his usual condition despite his physical handicap. Thus as his tale begins, he is on the road, having sighted two travelers named A and C, who meet each other briefly. Then Molloy decides to go to see his mother (a tricky proposition when we consider that our crippled hero intends to go there on bicycle), but he is arrested by a policeman. He is released after managing to utter his name, which he had forgotten, only to meet up with the law again when he runs over an old widow's dog. This time he is taken away by the widow rather than by the officer, but he manages to escape and soon finds himself on the coast, where he lays in a supply of "sucking-stones," pebbles he collects and sucks on in order to stave off hunger—or out of sheer compulsion. He spends pages on end describing the elaborate precautions he takes to ensure that he sucks all sixteen stones he possesses—shades of the fascination with permutations already operating in *Watt*. Soon Molloy's other leg starts to stiffen, but he betakes himself to a forest where he comes upon a variety of individuals: a shepherd, a guardian, and ultimately a charcoal-burner whom he kills with his crutches. Shortly thereafter he hears voices enjoining him to leave the forest without delay, and even more curiously he is surprised by the sound of a gong. He continues his journey, crawling now, and falls into a ditch at the edge of the forest. There we leave him, as his narrative ends. We never find out how he got to his mother's room.

It is then that a second account begins, the narrative by Moran, who is a kind of "private eye" working for a vast, undefined agency. A messenger named Gaber comes to him in his garden on a Sunday and instructs him to go off with his son on a search for Molloy. Moran never finds Molloy, but instead comes to resemble him more and more. In fact, the whole narrative can be read as the story of Moran's gradual metamorphosis into Molloy. As he sets out on his search for Molloy, his legs start atrophying, like Molloy's. He sends his son off to buy a bicycle, secondhand (one has the impression that the first owner should have been Molloy), and the boy abandons him. So Moran finds himself, like Molloy, alone in the forest. Partly paralyzed, sometimes crawling, he meets up with a series of individuals, one of whom he inexplicably murders, as Molloy killed the charcoal-burner. He too hears voices and a gong. His search ends when Gaber comes to him out of the blue, instructing him to return home. There he must write the account of his search, which is presumably the narrative we read—a strange report, containing personal and insubordinate comments that no practical-minded employee would ever include.

Let us now backtrack to Molly's episode with A and C, which some commentators have seen as an outline for the novel as a whole, sketching Moran's failed encounter with Molloy as well as their disastrous meetings with other individuals. The passage begins, "So I saw A and C going slowly towards each other, unconscious of what they were doing. It was on a road remarkably bare" (TN 8). A's and C's unconsciousness corresponds to the imperceptible movement of Molloy's ruminations as they slip from one concern to the other; the bareness of the road has its analogue in the smoothness of Molloy's language, its lack of embellishment, which carries us along the path of his obsessions. As we get lost in the text that we are forced to reread, so C "went with uncertain step and often stopped to look about him, like someone trying to fix landmarks in his mind, for one day perhaps he may have to retrace his steps" (TN 9).

Molloy sometimes confuses A and C; this merging, one of many in the text, figures our own confusion in attempting to follow Molloy's tale, as well as the later transformation of Moran into Molloy. An identification between Molloy and C is suggested as well when Molloy speaks of C's headgear:

> the hat, a town hat, an old-fashioned town hat, which the least gust would carry far away. Unless it was attached under the chin, by means of a string or an elastic. I took off my hat and looked at it. It is fastened, it has always been fastened, to my buttonhole, always the same buttonhole, at all seasons by a long lace. I am still alive then (TN 13–14).

Molloy calls C's hat not "his hat" but "the hat," and soon he begins to speak of "my hat," merging his with C's: the identification of C with Molloy proceeds through the hat. This fits in well with the importance of hats in Beckett generally. Beckett's protagonists often wear them; in *Malone Dies* an ass is photographed wearing one; and the very absence of this article in Murphy's wardrobe is commented upon, to the effect that he avoided wearing one because it reminded him painfully of the maternal caul. Most memorable, however, is Lucky's hat in *Waiting for Godot:* when he does not have it on, he ceases to think. A hat, of course, protects the head, but in Beckett it serves to keep one's mind working: Molloy knows he is alive because he still has his hat. But insofar as a hat can change wearers, can be transferred (as imperceptibly occurs in this passage), it shows how questionable that sense of self is. Therefore, Molloy attaches his hat with an elastic.

After the hat we come across another distinctive prop: the bicycle. In a well-known article on Beckett critic Hugh Kenner speaks of this vehicle as the Cartesian invention par excellence.[2] For Descartes the body, separate from the mind, works as a machine; thus a bicycle could be seen as an extension of the body not quite attached to it. But Molloy's bicycle—like his mind and body—is a strange machine, which runs against all logic: "It was a chainless bicycle, with a free-wheel, if such a bicycle exists" (TN 16). Though this cripple's bicycle and bicycle-riding may seem unrealistic, we are told not to worry about it: "I cannot stoop, neither can I kneel, because of my infirmity, and if I ever stoop, forgetting who I am, or kneel, make no mistake, it will not be me, but another" (TN 36).

Thus the narrator tells us that his story is not his own; instead, it generates itself, moving on its own much as a chainless bicycle would. Even the bicycle's presence is due to the narrative's relentless self-production. Molloy had no idea that this story would even include a bicycle: "So I got up, adjusted my crutches and went down to the road, where I found my bicycle (I didn't know I had one)" (TN 15–16). Molloy's feeling of estrangement from his own text shows up again when he hears voices in the forest, when he has trouble remembering his name, and when he refers to himself in the third person: "Chameleon in spite of himself, there you have Molloy, viewed from a certain angle" (TN 30). Thus he ends his narrative, after falling into the ditch: "Molloy could stay, where he happened to be" (TN 91).

The feeling that what occurs to oneself is happening to another, the ignorance of one's own story even as one tells it: this is the way we experience the repressed, according to Freud. Indeed, one of Molloy's major concerns is something repressed in the development of most individuals: anality. For example, a policeman stops Molloy because of the strange position he adopts on his bicycle and demands to see his papers. Molloy produces documentation of a surprising kind: "Now the only papers I carry with me are bits of newspaper to wipe myself, you understand, when I have a stool. [. . .] In a panic I took this paper from my pocket and thrust it under his nose" (TN 20). Excrement on paper is offered up as a significant document. Likewise, Molloy sees his writing as no more than blackening of paper:

> You would do better, at least no worse, to obliterate texts than to blacken margins, to fill in the holes of words till all is blank and flat and the whole ghastly business looks like what it is, senseless, speechless, issueless misery (TN 13).

The analogy between Molloy's blackened paper and used toilet tissue appears even more clearly in the original French: let the whole ghastly business, he says, look like what it is: "un non-sens cul et sans issue"—issueless and asslike (could one say *asinine?*) nonsense. In this respect it is interesting that in the original French, Beckett had named the two men Molloy sighted in the distance A and B; the change to A and C allows the association *caca* (childhood French for "excrement") to come in.

The obsession with excrement corresponds to the filthiness we would expect from a hobo like Molloy: "To him who has nothing it is forbidden not to relish filth" (TN 24). But Molloy points to a certain purity of the anus: the mouth ingests practically all that is put into it, but the anus expels all that is not itself. Thus the anus would be

> the true portal of our being and the celebrated mouth no more than the kitchen-door. Nothing goes in, or so little, that is not rejected on the spot, or very nearly. Almost everything revolts it that comes from without and what comes from within does not receive a very warm welcome either (TN 80).

This glorification of the anus shows how much Molloy embodies the repressed. It appears that he has realized his Oedipal desires, having slept with his mother; he would accept castration, the symbolic punishment for that act, claiming he would be glad "if they had removed a few testicles" from him (TN 35). Molloy is obsessed with one of the most basic things to be repressed: sexual difference. He seems unsure of the existence of the vagina, and wonders whether the women he knew were really men. He reports that his mother gave birth to him through the anus, and makes love to women through that orifice.

Molloy's obsession with the repressed has led many critics to see in him a representation of Moran's unconscious. Moran, the narrator of the second half of the novel, is the complete opposite of the tramp that Molloy is. He is a good burgher, respectful of religion, leading an eminently ordered life. After Molloy's confusing, seemingly endless, slightly obscene narrative, Moran's is at first reassuring. It proceeds in paragraphs of normal length and recounts an apparently less eccentric tale.

Yet immediately there are elements that undermine this impression of familiarity. For example, the organization that sends Moran off to search for Molloy has a theological dimension, recalling the troubling vision of bureaucracy in Kafka's novel *The Trial.* Moran's sense of obligation toward the employer goes beyond any simple fulfillment of duty and is dictated by an unquestionable imperative. His boss is named Youdi, a pejorative French term for Jew, which in this context might evoke the Hebrew God Yahweh. Moran prides himself on his knowledge of the Old Testament, and Youdi's messenger to Moran is named Gaber, reminiscent of the angel Gabriel.

The transmission of impenetrable commandments to Moran is repeated in Moran's relationship to his son, to whom he issues orders that must be obeyed. It occurs to him that the stringency of the journey might prove fatal to the boy, but Moran excuses himself in advance by thinking that Youdi commanded him to take his son along. The allusion to the binding of Isaac, the story of Abraham's near-sacrifice of his son, is clear.

This biblical episode is read in Christian tradition as a figure, an anticipation of the crucifixion, the sacrifice of Jesus for the sake of humankind. The partaking of the sacrificial victim is symbolized in the ceremony of Communion, and thus it becomes interesting that Moran is upset when the Sunday visit from Gaber keeps him from receiving the wafer at Mass. He must ask his priest for a private Communion:

> I said, Sunday for me without the Body and Blood is like—. He raised his hand. Above all no profane comparisons, he said. Perhaps he was thinking of the kiss without a moustache or beef without mustard. [. . .] I wondered if he had fed. I knew he was given to prolonged fasts, by way of mortification certainly, and then because his doctor advised it. Thus he killed two birds with one stone. Not a word to a soul, he said, let it remain between us and—. He broke off, raising a finger, and his eyes, to the ceiling. Heavens, he said, what is that stain? (TN 100)

The priest warns Moran not to mix the sacred and the nonsacred by making "profane comparisons," yet he does the same himself by fasting because it is good for his body as well as his soul, and by confusing the heavens with his ceiling. Such quotidian concerns were of course foreign to Molloy; in this way he was truly transcendent, even if his transcendence often bore on the repugnant. Thus critic Ludovic Janvier reads Moran's search for Molloy as the impossible striving of the immanent for the transcendent;[3] therefore, we need not be surprised that Moran never finds Molloy. Moran's encounter with Jesus during Communion is equally fruitless: he "felt like one who, having swallowed a pain-killer, is first astonished, then indignant, on obtaining no relief" (TN 102). The transcendent host is reduced to something banal: an analgesic.

The parallel between Moran's search for Molloy and his desire for Communion is far-reaching. Just as the Catholic ingests Jesus in the Eucharist and is supposed to imitate Christ in his life, so Moran incorporates Molloy, becoming like him. Moran never notices this resemblance, but in this way as well he rejoins Molloy's unconsciousness. His discourse begins to slip from him, leaving its reasonableness behind and revealing the Molloy-like ruminations beneath it:

> I still had a few hours left before dinner. I decided to make the most of them. Because after dinner I drowse. I took off my coat and shoes, opened my trousers and got in between the sheets. It is lying down, in the warmth, in the gloom, that I best pierce the outer turmoil's veil, discern my quarry, sense what course to follow, find peace in another's ludicrous distress. Far from the world, its clamours, frenzies, bitterness and dingy light, I pass judgment on it and on those, like me, who are plunged in it beyond recall, and on him who has need of me to be delivered, who cannot deliver myself. All is dark, but with that simple darkness that follows like a balm upon the great dismemberings. From their places masses move, stark as laws. Masses of what? One does not ask (TN 110).

At the beginning of this passage Moran is the sensible man who uses his time wisely; the orderliness of his life is suggested by the short, clear sentences; so sure is he of himself that he feels he has the right to judge others. As the passage goes on, the sentences get longer and more confusing until they approach senselessness. Soon Moran is talking of "masses," but of what even he does not know. His discourse escapes him no less than Molloy's did Molloy.

Despite the similarity between the two narratives Molloy's is placed under the sign of the mother, whereas

Moran's is dominated by the father figures Youdi and Moran himself. However, Molloy mentions at the beginning of his account that he may have a son somewhere, "nearly as old as [him]self" (TN 7), and later on he notes that his own mother would take him for his father. Thus Molloy is both father and son, and the same is true of Moran, who has given his son the same Christian name as himself: Jacques. Moreover, as a widower Moran is both father and mother to his boy; at one point he imagines attaching his son to himself by means of a long rope, suggestive of an umbilical cord.

Another area of convergence between Molloy and Moran is their sexuality. But here again what is expressed in Molloy's narrative is repressed in Moran's. If Molloy makes no secret of his enjoyment of anal eroticism, Moran only indulges in his under the guise of something medically useful, when he gives his son an enema:

> I withdrew the nozzle. Try and hold it, I said, don't stay sitting on the pot, lie flat on your stomach. We were in the bathroom. He lay down on the tiles, his big fat bottom sticking up. Let it soak well in, I said ["Laisse-le bien pénétrer," literally, *Let it penetrate well*]. What a day. I looked at the ash on my cigar. It was firm and blue (TN 118).

The symbolism of the cigar tip, firm and blue like the engorged glans of a penis, is clear. This scene is the repressed version of a homosexual and incestuous rape, reminding us of Molloy's anal penetration of several women and possibly some men, as well as of his sexual acts with his mother.

It is with respect to the relationship between Molloy's and Moran's narratives—whereby what is repressed by Malone is expressed by Molloy—that we can understand Moran's comment to the effect that "it was not for nothing I had studied the old testament" (TN 118). For what is symbolically portrayed in the Old Testament is realized in the New. Not only Abraham's near-sacrifice of his son but also Joseph's brothers' murderous longings toward Joseph followed by Joseph's rescue of them, and Moses' leading of his people followed by his being taken up into God's arms, foretell aspects of Jesus' crucifixion and resurrection. In Christian terms the Old Testament is truly meaningful only in reference to the New; the later book logically—though not chronologically—precedes the earlier one. Likewise, Moran's narrative takes on its full sense with respect to Molloy's; that is no doubt why Beckett put Moran's tale after Molloy's, even though some critics have said that Molloy as the object of the search should appear after the searcher has presented his account. Moreover, in terms of its primordial elements—the obsession with anality and filth and the freely associative ruminations—Molloy's tale is prior to Moran's more civilized discourse.

Moran's narrative functions not only as an allegory of Molloy's as the Old Testament functions as an allegory of the New; it also serves as an allegory of our own attempt to read Molloy's narrative. For just as we must figure out from Molloy's ramblings what he is trying to say, so Moran attempts to interpret Molloy on the basis of scanty information. "I knew then about Molloy," says Moran, "without however knowing much about him." He continues:

He hastened incessantly on [...]. Now a prisoner, he hurled himself at I know not what narrow confines, and now, hunted, he sought refuge near the centre.

He panted. He had only to rise up within me for me to be filled with panting (TN 113).

Moran's description of Molloy's movements is not only accurate as such but also applies to the movement of Molloy's text, which circles around one obsession only to recoil from it. His panting along with Molloy corresponds to the reader's identification with the hobo despite his repugnance. The interpretation of Moran as a figure for the reader is supported by the fact that his name is an anagram of *roman,* the French word for "novel." Anagram-hunting is not foreign to the text: Moran mentions in passing a character Obidil, a word that is literally the mirror image of "libido." This disfigurement of libido corresponds to Moran's repression of sexuality, to his fixation on the punishing father that makes him teach his son to abhor the body.

If Moran never realizes he has become like Molloy, this is because he, like the reader, cannot admit he can be so abject. But as French writer George Bataille notes in his article on this text, Molloy "follows us no less faithfully than our shadow."[4] We are hounded by the image of the vagabond because we see ourselves in him but must remain blind to this awareness to keep our sense of self. We cannot grasp the tramp's being, for his words can only be emptiness compared to the supposed fullness of the language we use. Hence Bataille calls his article "Molloy's Silence," implying that we cannot understand Molloy's words.

Incomprehensibility is a theme in *Molloy*. For example, when Moran returns home from his abortive search for Molloy, he finds his bees dead—the bees that in their busyness symbolized Moran's work ethic, abandoned as he was transfigured into Molloy. Moran had earlier described how he attempted to decipher the bees' dance, only to realize that he never could: "And I said, with rapture, Here is something I can study all my life, and never understand" (TN 169). Moran here feels like the reader, who can study the complexities of *Molloy* for a lifetime without ever fully understanding it. But as Moran contemplates this incomprehensibility with rapture, so do we.

Molloy too has an experience of incomprehension when he finds himself at the widow Lousse's home. Lousse has a parrot, of whom Molloy says, "I understood him better than his mistress. I don't mean I understood him better than she understood him, I mean I understood him better than I understand her" (TN 37). Molloy might understand the parrot, but there is something incomprehensible for us: in the French original Molloy remarks upon the fact that the bird speaks French. It is as though in this text written in French everybody were actually speaking English—which indeed would have to be the case. Molloy and Moran are Irish names, Moran chomps on Irish stew, the landscape with its peat is typical Irish, and Molloy tells us that "da, in my part of the world, means father" (TN 17). That these Irishmen, like their creator, should write in French is not the least of the text's riddles; the book is even more inexplicable in its original French than in English.

Malone Dies

Beckett's next work, *Malone Dies,* also begins with an *m;* the French title is even alliterative: *Malone meurt.* Like Molloy and Moran, Malone is a semiparalyzed narrator; he is old, bedridden, in some kind of institution. He assures us it is not a hospital or insane asylum, but his very insistence suggests it might be such a place. As he awaits his imminent death, he writes a diary. His plan is to describe his present state, tell some stories, and draw up the inventory of his possessions.

Malone's situation shows how much he has inherited from Molloy. Like his predecessor, who lived in the room he had inherited from his mother, Malone came into his room upon the death of its previous inhabitant. Molloy says of his room: "I don't know how I got there. Perhaps in an ambulance, certainly a vehicle of some kind" (TN 7), and Malone says of his: "I do not remember how I got here. In an ambulance perhaps, a vehicle of some kind certainly" (TN 183). The woman who comes to take care of him and whom he has trouble understanding reminds one of the widow who lavished care on Molloy. Like Molloy, Malone had walked all his days previous to his inhabitation of this room, perhaps in a forest. There he might have been "stunned with a blow, on the head" (TN 183), now less like Molloy or Moran than like one of the solitary walkers they attacked on their journeys. Thus Malone partakes of the identities of several of the characters in *Molloy,* just as they had partaken of each others' selves. Also similar to the previous volume there is confusion not only of characters but of sexes. Originally Malone plans to

write four stories—"One about a man, another about a
woman, a third about a thing and finally one about an
animal, a bird probably"—whereupon he decides to "put
the man and the woman in the same story, there is so
little difference between a man and a woman" (TN 181).

Malone begins his first story—and it will be the
only one he will have time to tell before his death—
about a character who resembles him all too well. Like
Moran incorporating Molloy, Malone's character takes
on Malone's being. Moreover, as Moran's son bears the
same name as he, so Malone tells us his alter ego's
"name is Saposcat. Like his father's. [...] His friends
call his Sapo. What friends? I don't know" (TN 186).
This passage illustrates another strategy Beckett had
already used: the generation of narrative through linguistic reflex. Molloy, upon recounting that he possessed a bicycle, is surprised to learn he owned one;
now Malone, upon mentioning Sapo's friends, is unaware he had any. But there is a different in tone between the two passages. Molloy is exuberant as he discovers his own narrative unfolding before his eyes, whereas
Malone is indifferent. He interrupts his tale with remarks like "What tedium" (TN 187, 189) and "This is
awful" (TN 191).

So often does he editorialize that his commentar-
ies take up as much space as his story. In many
sections of the book paragraphs or even sentences alternate, with one recounting the story of Saposcat and the
next reflecting on it and changing it. Thus whereas
Moran's narrative functioned as a reading of Molloy's
narrative in an unconscious, implicit manner, it is in
a literal, explicit sense that Malone reads the story of
Saposcat. And like Moran's interpretation of Molloy,

Malone's interpretation of his own tale coincides with ours, as when he remarks on how uneventful it is.

Another similarity between *Molloy* and *Malone Dies* concerns their alter egos. Molloy and Malone are tramps consigned to rooms; Moran and Saposcat are middle-class. But there are some differences. Moran is the firmly entrenched petit-bourgeois father, whereas Saposcat is alienated, like Moran's son. He is the ungifted scion of a couple who dream of one thing: pushing their offspring into a liberal profession so as to assure themselves of a comfortable retirement. Here as well one remarks the difference in tone between the two books. *Molloy* holds up Moran's hypocrisy to frolicsome ridicule, especially in the scene with the priest, while *Malone Dies* subjects the Saposcats to more blasé irony. Their life is said to be "full of axioms, of which one at least established the criminal absurdity of a garden without roses and with its paths and lawns uncared for" (TN 187). So worn out and conventionalized is their conversation that "they made use of the spoken word in much the same way as the guard of a train makes use of his flags" (TN 188). Their son's language is no more felicitous, since he fails his oral as well as his written exams. Such an unhappy relationship with language reminds us of Beckett's own dilemma as he shifts from English to French and back again.

Having so little success in his parents' world, Sapo spends time at the home of a nearby peasant family, named Louis in *Malone meurt* and Lambert in *Malone Dies*—perhaps a reference to Balzac's novel *Louis Lambert*. Malone describes these peasants not to praise rural life but to show its tedium: no idyll is possible in Beckett's world. Thus Madame Louis/Lambert is shown sorting out lentils, dropping them on the floor, and giving up the task. This episode corresponds to Molloy's careful distribution of the pebbles he sucks, but again in the first novel the tone is exuberant, whereas in the second it is lackluster.

After such undistinguished beginnings Sapo disappears for several pages during which Malone muses on his writing, his surroundings, his possessions, his existence—such as it is. Suddenly Sapo reemerges as an old man on a bench, but Malone can no longer tolerate calling him that; he redubs him Macmann. If Saposcat was a petit-bourgeois creature like Moran, Saposcat's alter ego Macmann is a tramp like Moran's alter ego Molloy. This new vagabond too wears a hat attached with a string and crawls on the ground. His most memorable adventure occurs at the end of the book. There Macmann, like his creator Malone, finds himself in an institution; only in Macmann's case it is definitely a mental institution, as at the end of *Murphy*. Macmann has a love affair with his attendant, a woman named Moll—which makes one think not only of "gun moll" but also of Molloy and his gender confusion. Moll dies; in her place as attendant comes a man named Lemuel, who murders with an ax all in his care, including Macmann. Shortly after his creature's demise, Malone dies while writing. The book ends in mid-sentence:

> never anything
> there
> any more (TN 288).

Let us consider for a moment why one writes. The most obvious answer is to achieve immortality. For a writer immortality implies the possibility of narrating his own death. If he can write *I am dying, I die, I am dead,* then he has survived death, he has become immortal. Yet even though I have just written *I die,* these words cannot be uttered in any true sense. The sentence *I die* must be a fiction; the *I* spoken of can only be an unreal character, someone other than myself, a *he.* Thus even though Malone is a first-person narrator, Beckett does not call the book *I Die* but *Malone Dies.* Doing so, he points to the unfulfillable wish upon which literature is based, the wish to narrate one's own death.

Malone's desire to write the words *I die* is implicit from the book's first sentence, which reads, "I shall soon be quite dead at last in spite of all." The French opening, "Je serai quand même bientôt tout à fait mort enfin," includes the verb form "je serai mort," which means not only *I shall be dead,* as Beckett translates it, but also *I shall have died.* The future perfect is known to Beckett's public from the play *Happy Days,* where the protagonist says time and again, "This *will have been* a happy day"; "This *will have been* another happy day" (HD 40, 47–48, 64). This verb tense is as close as we can ever get to living the present, for we are never conscious of actually experiencing anything. Even while we experience it, we are aware solely that we *shall have experienced* it; the present does not exist for us as such, but as a past in the future. This is all the more true of the impossible present tense *I die;* the nearest we can get to saying it is *I shall have died.* Hence Malone is afraid that he will "rater mon décès" (*Malone meurt* 12). This is translated by Beckett as "make a mess of my decease" (TN 182), but it could mean *miss*

72

my decease. This fear is justified, for it would be impossible for Malone to enact his "plan [...] to [...] die alive" (TN 209), and thus write *I die*.

Yet Beckett heroes do not limit themselves to the possible. The paralyzed Molloy performs acrobatics on his chainless bicycle, and Malone will write without anything to write on: "In vain I grope, I cannot find my exercise-book. But I still have the pencil in my hand" (TN 208). The pencil assumes a symbolic function. At first a vulgar phallic symbol—he sucks on its ends as Molloy sucked his stones—it soon becomes more interesting:

> My pencil. It is a little Venus, still green no doubt, with five or six facets, pointed at both ends [...]. I use the two points turn and turn about, sucking them frequently, I love to suck. [...] The strange thing is I have another pencil, made in France, a long cylinder hardly broached, in the bed with me somewhere I think (TN 222–23).

Malone has two pencils, a nearly new French one and an older one, overused—perhaps an English one. For "pencils" we can read Beckett's two tongues, the English he had tired of and the French he had just started using. We need not be surprised that Malone uses the "English" pencil in this text originally written in French. Like his predecessors in *Molloy* he is an English-speaker, and French for him is a foreign tongue that he almost wishes he knew less well. In a sentence deleted from the English translation Malone says of Madame Louis's arms: "Elle les écartait de ses flancs, je dirais brandissait si j'ignorais encore mieux le génie de votre langue" (*Malone meurt* 46), which can translate as *she*

73

*moved them away from her sides, I would say bran-
dished them if I knew even less well the spirit of your
language.*

Malone may be Irish, but some of his points of
reference are French. Thus on the first page he writes
of the holidays he might live past this year: "Perhaps
I shall survive Saint John the Baptist's Day and even
the Fourteenth of July, festival of freedom. Indeed I
would not put it past me to pant on to the Transfiguration, not to speak of the Assumption" (TN 179). Bastille
Day (July 14) and Assumption Day (August 15) are
French national holidays. The description of Bastille
Day as the "festival of freedom" is ironic; there is little
festive in this book, and the paralyzed Malone is hardly
the picture of freedom. John the Baptist (his day is
June 24) died decapitated; headlessness is, figuratively,
the fate of all Beckett's heroes who ramble on. Malone
says, "At each fresh attempt I lost my head" (TN 195),
the narrator of *Texts for Nothing* asks, "What's the
matter with my head, I must have left it in Ireland, in
a saloon" (STN 113), and the French Unnamable will
remark that he has never had a head ("jamais eu [...]
de tête" [*L'Innommable* 65]). The Transfiguration (taking place on August 6 and marking Jesus' revelation
of himself as God) and the Assumption (which com-
memorates Mary's ascension to heaven) address even
more explicitly the fates of Beckett's characters. Moran *assumes* Molloy's identity, Molloy is Moran *transfigured* into a transcendent being, Malone is Molloy
and Moran changed into a moribund.

In turn Malone wishes to transform himself into
another; hence his story of Saposcat, "that child I might
have been" and no doubt was (TN 208). Yet he wishes

74

to believe that "nothing is less like me that this patient, reasonable child," and that his writing is concerned "not with me, but with another" (TN 193, 195).
Were Malone to become another, he could then utter
the sentence *he dies* in such a way that it would mean
I die. Thus toward the end of the text Malone writes,
"I shall say I no more" (TN 283), and writes instead of
his alter ego Macmann's demise—in order to narrate
his own death.

Yet Malone need not refer to himself as *he* in order
to make himself into another. The simple use of his
name would effect that. To say *I am Samuel,* for example, implies that for others I am not *I* but another: for
each of them they are their own *I* and I am Samuel,
not *I*. Thus when the narrator of *Malone Dies* tells us
his name, he uses the word "Malone" as though it des-
ignated a third person—and he evokes his death at the
same time. He speaks of the "conclusion of the whole
sorry business, I mean the business of Malone (since
that is what I am called now)" (TN 222). It is interesting
that Malone waits practically until the middle of the
book to provide his name, the term by which others can
designate him. It is as though he needed to approach
his death to make himself other than himself in reality
and not only through his creatures Saposcat and Macmann:
"on the threshold of being no more I succeed in being
another" (TN 194).

Yet Malone need not use his name or the third-
person pronoun to see himself die, as one sees another
die; this is evident on a page where Malone writes, "I
fear I must have fallen asleep again," and a few lines
later, "I have just written, I fear I must have fallen,
etc." (TN 208). In the first sentence the first *I—I* who

fear I have fallen asleep again—is the present *I,* the narrator; the second *I,* the one who slept, the one about whom the narrative *I* is speaking, functions as a sort of character existing in the past. Yet as soon as the sentence is uttered or written, the first *I* also becomes a preexistent character. Thus in the second sentence, "I have just written, I fear I must have fallen, etc.," the *I* of "I fear" has become a character, and only the first *I,* who says he has "just written," is the narrator. But once that sentence is uttered or set down on paper, that *I* too becomes a character other than the narrator. The narrator departs from that *I* and returns in its next occurrence. As the French philosopher Jacques Derrida writes: "My death is structurally necessary to the pronouncing of the *I.*"[5]

Likewise, in enumerating his possessions Malone speaks of himself as another. His inventory is similar to a last will and testament, that document by which one imagines oneself dead and dispossessed. Evoking his pots—a word that must remind us of the passage in *Watt* where Watt loses his identity as the pots lose theirs—Malone writes. "They are not mine, but I say my pots, as I say my bed, my window, as I say me" (TN 252).

Molloy had also planned "to draw up the inventory of [his] goods and possessions" (TN 14) but never gotten around to it, perhaps because he discovered that to name a thing somehow erases it: "There could be no things but nameless things, no names but thingless names"; "To restore silence is the role of objects" (TN 31, 13). Malone makes a similar discovery: "My notes have a curious tendency [...] to annihilate all they purport to record" (TN 259). It is as though the word—

especially the written word in its permanence—were substituted for the more mobile object. Thus if Malone writes about himself, his writing takes the place of himself. It is often said that literature makes the absent present, but in *Malone Dies* we see literature making the present absent. Thus Malone speaks of "the blessedness of absence" (TN 222) and asks his last visitor for an eraser in addition to a pencil lead.

That writing effaces the objects it evokes is symbolized in the final pages of the novel, where we meet the attendant named Lemuel, whom we may see as a figure for the writer Beckett, named Samuel. If Malone—and by extension Beckett—"annihilate all they purport to record" (including themselves: is not Samuel Beckett for us the works he wrote, more than the man he was?), so Lemuel murders all the patients in his care. Lemuel also deals a few blows to his own head with the blunt side of a hammer, but on the others he uses a hatchet, in the French original an *hache*. *Hache* is also French for the letter *h:* the writer kills with an *h,* as though writing were literally annihilation.

During this murderous rampage a delirious Englishman ("l'Anglais" in the French text, a "Saxon" in the English version) calls out, "Nice work, sir, nice work!" (TN 287, in English in the original)—a comment that can be applied as well to the text of *Malone Dies,* which makes short order of all it is about. As Malone says:

> All is pretext, Sapo and the birds, Moll, the peasants, those who in the towns seek one another out and fly from one another, my doubts which do not interest me, my situation, my possessions, pretext for not

coming to the point, the abandoning, the raising of the arms and going down (TN 276).

Note that this passage begins, "All is pretext, Sapo and the *birds*." Birds appear in *Malone Dies* more than in any other work by Beckett. Malone had planned to tell the story of a bird; Sapo "loved the flight of the hawk" and had "gull's eyes" (TN 191, 192); the Louis family chases wild birds off their land and chickens out of their kitchen; Malone mentions "millet grains beloved of birds" as a possible topic of discussion (TN 225); Macmann is "by temperament more reptile than bird" (TN 243); "a little bird tells" Malone that he will not finish his inventory (TN 249); birds are "numerous and varied" where Macmann goes for an outing near his institution (TN 276). A bird also figures as a writing implement: Saposcat's parents give him a Blackbird-brand fountain pen the day before his examination. In that passage the word *bec,* meaning "beak," appears, which allows us to read the birds as instances of *Bec*kett's signature (*Malone meurt* 60). The use of a bird as an emblem has a literary pedigree: Kafka's name in Czech meant "jackdaw," and his father's business stationery portrayed that bird. (For more about the resonance of Beckett's name as *little beak,* see chapter 1 above.)

While the parrot in *Molloy* spoke French and English, the same animal in *Malone Dies* knows some Latin. Malone's friend Jackson has a parrot that reproduces the first three words of a philosophical maxim, *Nihil in intellectu quod non prius in sensu* ("There is nothing in the mind that was not first in the senses"). According to this doctrine we are aware of nothing that we have not experienced directly, for there is no inborn knowledge. Reality is inscribed on the tabula rasa, the empty slate, that the newborn's mind is held to be. But in the parrot's version of the formula, consisting only of *Nihil in intellectu,* the tabula rasa remains blank. What should have been written on it is produced instead as an insistent squawking: "These first three words the bird managed well enough, but the celebrated restriction was too much for it, all you heard was a series of squawks" (TN 218).

In the French original the text mimics rather than describes the parrot's squawking. It reproduces it as *couah,* sounding like the Latin *quod* and the French *quoi,* both of which mean "what": "Ces trois premiers mots, l'oiseau les prononçait bien, mais la célèbre restriction ne passait pas, on n'entendait que couah couah couah couah couah" (*Malone meurt* 72). One of the most important philosophical debates of all times—tabula rasa versus innate knowledge—is reduced here to "a matter of fundamental sounds," to quote once again the formula Beckett used to describe his own works. This is similar to the fate that befalls another science when Molloy counts his farts and declares: "Extraordinary how mathematics helps you to know yourself" (TN 30).

The parrot repeating the maxim is typical of the fragmentation of high culture in *Malone Dies.* Malone trots out other bits of learning when he quotes three words from the Latin author Lucretius (TN 218), when he informs us of the etymology of the month of May (TN 234), and when he mentions the "great heat" of the seventh century (TN 245) and "the Colossus of Memnon, dearly loved son of Dawn" (TN 227). The rustle of Macmann's coat, "like certain curtains" along the floor (TN 227), may be an allusion to Theodor Fontane's novel *Effi Briest,* referred to by name in *All That Fall* and *Krapp's Last Tape* (CSP 29, 62). Painting crops up as well, as when Malone speaks of the nightscapes of Caspar David Friedrich and of the trompe-l'oeil in "Tiepolo's ceiling at Würzburg, what a tourist I must have been" (TN 235).

Tourism is the trivialization of travel, and thus it partakes of Malone's tendency to focus on tidbits of culture. Culture functions in *Malone Dies* as residue at best, and garbage at worst. An example of culture turned rubbish is an allusion Malone makes to a passage from the nineteenth-century German dramatist Franz Grillparzer: "des langen Sommers Freuden" *(the joys of the long summer).*[6] Malone incorporates this phrase, translated almost exactly, into an idyllic description of Macmann's surroundings: "These leaves [...] are perhaps no longer the first of the year, barely green, but old leaves that have known the long joys of summer"—but then he adds that these leaves "now are good for nothing but to lie rotting in a heap" (TN 231).

Malone, whose name resonates as *me alone,* speaks of "extremes [...] of solitude" and longs for companions "that would never have [him]" (TN 191, 193). His dismissal of culture suggests he cannot even have friends in the form of other books and authors, for his tales are too aberrant:

> They will not be the same kind of stories as hitherto [...]. They will be neither beautiful nor ugly, they will be calm, there will be no ugliness or beauty or fever in them any more, they will be almost lifeless, like the teller (TN 180).

In *Malone Dies* we see the teller go from the "almost lifeless" to the "lifeless." One presumes then that the tales will end: "Then it will be all over with the Murphys [. . .], Molloys, Morans and Malones, unless it goes on beyond the grave" (TN 236). A posthumous voice may well be what we hear in Beckett's next novel.

The Unnamable

This work is the logical outcome of the process begun by the previous volumes of the trilogy. In *Molloy* the first half, Molloy's tale, is followed by Moran's narrative, which functions as a reading of it. In *Malone Dies* the story and its commentary are not polarized: nearly every paragraph that tells Sapo/Macmann's tale is followed by another where Malone gives his reaction to it. In *The Unnamable,* almost devoid of paragraphs, the division between story and commentary disappears. The slight elements of plot it possesses drown in the narrator's endless self-commentary and self-questioning, which become the Unnamable's true story.

The best introduction to *The Unnamable* remains its opening words: "Where now? Who now? When now?" These are not rhetorical questions. They remain unanswered and unanswerable: for the narrator they are examples of "aporia," a logical difficulty to which there is no solution (TN 291). Despite the ultimate unanswerability, however, the narrator takes stabs at his questions. Like us he is trying to read his own text, even as he produces it, and like us he comes up with very little he can be sure of.

Regarding the first question, "Where now?" the narrator finds himself in a gray place, sometimes brightly illuminated, sometimes dark, and almost always silent. He calls his abode a "parlour" (TN 410), and the use of this word, from the French *parler* meaning "to speak," emphasizes the Unnamable's nonstop discourse. At several points he compares his habitation to hell, though in a typically Beckettian movement of self-contradiction, which the Unnamable calls "affirmations and negations invalidated as uttered" (TN 291), he also likens it to paradise. These may be allusions to *The Inferno* and *The Paradiso* by Dante, who figured so prominently in the essay Beckett wrote on Joyce.

The Unnamable never makes it clear whether he actually is in the other world, but if he were, it would follow that he is now dead. Thus the question "When now?" has the possible answer "after life." Malone wished to write "I die"; the Unnamable could well be his continuation, the narrator who could say, "I have died." The dead narrator was already exploited by Beckett in a 1946 story, *Le Calmant (The Calmative)*, that began with the words, "I don't know when I died" (STN 27). The Unnamable says of dying that "it has happened to me many times already" (TN 342). We cannot even be sure whether he is dead now: he informs us that after each death he was quickly resurrected.

The possibility that the Unnamable's narrative continues Malone's suggests "Malone" as an answer to the question "Who now?" The Unnamable assures us that Malone *is* there, revolving around him like a planet around its sun; we can imagine that the Unnamable is the interior voice that had spoken forth from Malone. But the Unnamable informs us that this satellite may actually be Molloy wearing Malone's hat; as in *Molloy*, the hat emerges as the flawed guarantor of identity.

The confusion between Molloy and Malone leads the Unnamable to declare that "they are all here, at least from Murphy on" (TN 293). This continues a technique in *Molloy,* where Moran mentioned characters from Beckett's earlier books. Such cross-references confer upon Beckett's writings the appearance of a universe unto itself. Other authors had employed the same strategy before: in France Balzac comes to mind. Yet there is an important difference between the two uses of the same method. In Balzac's prose it is as though one work could not contain the variegated world of the author's imagination, whereas in Beckett's sparse works the same characters turn up time and again because human possibilities are fundamentally limited.

Though the Unnamable says that "they are all here, at least from Murphy on," these characters never converse with him or keep him company. His relationship to them resembles the one between Malone and Sapo/Macmann: creator and creature do not exist on the same plane. Yet whereas Malone is conscious that he has created Sapo/Macmann in a fictional sense, the Unnamable sometimes speaks of his creatures as though he were a divine creator and they really existed. When he says, "It is no doubt time I gave a companion to Malone" (TN 296), this reminds us of the verse from Genesis where God creates Eve for Adam: "I will make him a help meet for him" (2:18). And when the Unnamable asks, "Why did I have myself represented in the midst of men, the light of day?" (TN 297), it is almost as if he were God speaking of transfiguring himself into Jesus.

The title, *The Unnamable,* reinforces this divine aspect of the narrator, for in several mystical traditions God's name cannot be uttered. Insofar as the Unnamable talks endlessly, compulsively, his speech functions as an unfortunate version of God's infinity, of his eternal voice, just as the devil is the negative of God. In fact, in one of the passages where the Unnamable compares his abode to hell, he draws an explicit analogy between his own and Satan's eternity: "Hell itself, although eternal, dates from the revolt of Lucifer. It is therefore permissible, in the light of this distant analogy, to think of myself as being here forever, but not as having been here forever" (TN 295–96).

Like Malone, who finds that despite his wishes his character Sapo/Macmann resembles him, so the Unnamable occasionally identifies with his creatures, especially with one who changes in name. This alter ego is first called Basil, then Mahood, and finally Worm. Like Saposcat and Macmann, these names have significance. Basil indicates the character's *base*ness. Manhood suggests an attempt to raise this creature to the status of man, a failed attempt since this manhood is castrated of its central letter, *n:* the Unnamable's creation of man is flawed, much as one could argue God's attempt is. Finally, the name Worm shows Ma(n)hood's redescent into vileness.

It is thanks to this diversely named character that we have the only elements of a story in *The Unnamable* other than the purely obsessive questioning by the narrator of who is he. The narrator recounts what occurred to him during the years when he "took [himself] for Mahood" (TN 317). He was on a world tour, during which he became dismembered: "Perhaps I had left my leg behind in the Pacific," he tells us with his typical uncertainty (TN 317). This traveler returns home,

84

longing to embrace his children including those "born in [his] absence" (TN 317): this abandonment of paternity can be likened to the Unnamable's refusal to endow his own account with certainty and authority. Unfortunately, Mahood finds all his relatives dead of poisoning, after having ingested spoiled canned goods. Hardly a traditional story, despite the rhetorical flourish that ends it: "Would I not have been more likely [...] to devour what remained of the fatal corned-beef?" (TN 324). (This last expression is identical—and more humorous—in the original French: "N'aurais-je pas plutôt [...] englouti ce qui restait du fatal corned-beef?")

Mahood's physical dismemberment, corresponding to the disjointed storytelling, continues as he loses (he knows not how) his other leg and both arms. We now find our quadriplegic narrator in a jar, cared for by the proprietress of a greasy-spoon restaurant near a slaughterhouse. Like Sapo/Macmann and Basil/Mahood/Worm the proprietress is unstably named: she is alternately called Marguerite and Madeleine. The Unnamable serves her in ways both utilitarian and aesthetic: in his jar he adorns the entrance to her restaurant, the menu is attached to him, and the excrement that accumulates beneath him fertilizes the vegetable garden. The Unnamable surpasses in abjection Beckett's other creatures: the smelly Molloy, the crawling Moran, the invalid Malone, and the bag-man Macmann. Here we detect another sense of the word *unnamable* and even more of the French title *L'Innommable:* "unspeakable, filthy."

Distasteful as the Unnamable is in this incarnation, he still imagines love. For the proprietress of the restaurant empties his receptacle "punctually and with-

out complaint, beyond an occasional good-natured re-
flection to the effect that I was a nasty old pig [...].
Without perhaps having exactly won her heart it was
clear that I did not leave her indifferent" (TN 328). As
in all love stories there is imperfect communication.
Marguerite/Madeleine covers Mahood up in the snow,
and Mahood would like to receive such treatment more
often. Apparently dispossessed of speech—he who speaks
compulsively for 150 pages!—the narrator tries to make
her understand his wish by moving his head and spit-
ting. She interprets this to mean that he wanted to be
covered less—"just the reverse of the truth. But credit
where credit is due, we made a balls of it between us,
I with my signs and she with her reading of them" (TN
329–30). This ironic comment can be applied as well to
the Unnamable emitting signs—words—and the reader
trying to interpret them.

It is at this point that the narrator changes Mahood's name to Worm, though in typical self-contradiction he will occasionally still speak of Mahood. With
the exception of passing reference to this character's
speech or silence, presence or absence, crawling or resting, we are no longer treated to anecdotes about him.
There is little more than the insistent questioning by
the narrative voice as to who or what he himself is. Is
he an eardrum, technically called a "tympanum" (TN
383)? Is he "a drying sperm, in the sheets of an innocent boy" (TN 379)? Is he "words among words, or silence in the midst of silence" (TN 388)? Is the best pronoun
for him *I, he, it,* or *they* (TN 355, 382, 403)? Henceforth,
the only thing that resembles a story occurs a few pages
before the end, when stories as such and happy endings

are mocked. Speaking of a couple he has vaguely alluded to, the Unnamable says:

> They love each other, marry, in order to leave each other better, more conveniently, he goes to the wars, he dies at the wars, she weeps, with emotion, at having loved him, at having lost him, yep, marries again, in order to love again, more conveniently again, they love each other, you love as many times as necessary, as necessary in order to be happy (TN 406).

The happy ending reveals itself not to be the end; the story goes on: "You love as many times as necessary, as necessary in order to be happy, he comes back, the other comes back, from the wars, he didn't die at the wars after all" (TN 406). This antistory continues for some twenty more lines. It reflects the text as a whole, a voice almost devoid of stories that speaks nevertheless.

The Unnamable abandons the tale of his alter ego because he ultimately rejects the notion that he was ever Basil, Mahood, Worm, or any other character: "I am neither, I needn't say, Murphy, nor Watt, nor Mercier, nor—no, I cannot even bring myself to name them" (TN 326). Yet the phrase by which the Unnamable seeks to distance himself from the others—"I cannot even bring myself to *name* them"—reveals that they are as unnamable as he; and even as he resists the idea that he could speak of himself in "the same foul breath as [his] creatures," he goes on to suggest that their existence is superior to his: "I alone am man and all the rest divine" (TN 300). Malone, even as he revolves around him subserviently like a planet around its sun, suddenly looms "impassive": he is "the god" (TN 300). Likewise, Mahood may well be the "master" (TN 311). If the Unnamable once led us to believe it was his voice speaking through Malone, now others seem to speak through the Unnamable: "I say what I'm told to say"; "Who is talking, not I [. . .] where are the others, it's they are talking" (TN 382, 385–86). (The feeling of speaking others' words allows the Unnamable to say that he is using a foreign language, the implications of which were discussed in chapter 1 above.)

Are the others who speak through the Unnamable the creatures he has invented and lost control of? At times this seems to be the case, as when "he says Murphy, or Molloy, I forget, as if I were Malone" (TN 403; of course, we would expect to read: *he says Murphy, or Molloy, I forget, as if I were Murphy, or Molloy;* by putting Malone's name in the place of Murphy's and Molloy's, the Unnamable stresses the interchangeability of all the characters with the initial *m*). Self-contradictorily, the Unnamable also suggests that the agency who speaks through him is nameless and no more reducible to "Mahood and Co[mpany]" (TN 346) than it is to himself: "It's always he who speaks, Mercier never spoke, Moran never spoke, I never spoke, I seem to speak, that's because he says I as if he were I" (TN 403).

We get lost in all these *it*'s, *he*'s and *I*'s, and in a typical moment of self-commentary the Unnamable points out: "It's the fault of the pronouns" (TN 404). The pronoun most responsible for this state of affairs is *I,* which the Unnamable, like his predecessor Malone, would like to give up altogether: "I shall not say I again, ever again, it's too farcical. I shall put in its place, whenever I hear it, the third person, if I think of it" (TN 355). The

I is insufferable, for one cannot stop saying *I* even when one plans to, as happens in the sentence just quoted: after the Unnamable declares he will henceforth replace *I* with *he,* he adds, automatically, "if I think of it."

The uncontrollability of one's own speech is not the only hateful thing about the *I*. Another of its unpleasant aspects becomes clear when the Unnamable declares that he has had "enough of this cursed first person" (TN 343). In French, this reads "assez de cette putain de première personne." Although *putain,* when used as a swear word, loses some force of its primary meaning of "whore," we can nonetheless read this expression literally as *enough of this whore of a first person*. In a sense the pronoun *I* does prostitute itself, for it goes with whoever employs it. Anyone can say *I* to refer to him- or herself. As the Unnamable puts it, the other "says I as if he were I" (TN 403). Thus the *I,* apparently the most personal of pronouns, does not belong to the speaker: *I* is not the name of the person who speaks. Here we can counter those readers who would reduce the Unnamable to a figure for the author, as though Beckett were the *I* speaking through the characters. If the pronoun *I* cannot be permanently attributed to any individual, we cannot identify the unstable *I* in this book with Beckett.

The unassignability of the *I* leads the Unnamable to say, "There is no name for me, no pronoun for me, all the trouble comes from that" (TN 404). Indeed, "all the trouble"—the entirety of this problematic text—comes from the impasse of the self who accepts as his own name neither the *I* nor any of the names that have been given him ("Mahood and Company"). It is in this sense that the speaker in this book is truly unnamable. Critics call him the Unnamable as though that were his name, but this is only for "the sake of clarity," as he himself would say (TN 295). Nowhere in the text—except in the title—is he called that, and one should savor the paradox that consists in naming something *The Unnamable*.

This word sounds like "innumerable," and the original title, *L'Innommable,* bears an even closer resemblance to the French word for innumerable, *innombrable,* which occurs twice in the text (*L'Innommable* 32, 156). In English it is translated as "numberless" (TN 306, 380), and numberlessness can be related to the bad infinity of the pronoun *I,* which can be used by anyone who speaks. As the narrator says: "There might be a hundred of us and still we'd lack the hundred and first"; "I could employ fifty wretches for this sinister operation and still be short of a fifty-first" (TN 339, 338). In the French original (*L'Innommable* 132) this relationship is expressed algebraically: "Ils seraient x qu'on aurait besoin d'un x-et-unième" (*there could be x of them and still we'd lack the (x + 1)th).* This formula bears not only on the numberless speakers but also on the terrible repetitiousness of the work. Though the Unnamable may have been told what to say "a hundred times," he needs to be told "a hundred and one, this time I'll try and pay attention" (TN 313).

Thus if the Unnamable constantly says the same thing, it is because the others who speak through him make him repeat. He claims his desire is to fall silent, but before he can do that, he must acquit himself of a "task, which consists in speaking of oneself" (TN 311). We see why he cannot comply with this obligation if we consider that both the speaking subject (the *I*) and one's various ego identifications ("Mahood and Company") are alienations from oneself. However, there is a way out. The Unnamable achieves silence, even when he apparently goes on speaking. Precisely by repeating himself, he comes to *say nothing* in a figurative sense, insofar as repetition wears meaning from words. This becomes clear in a compulsively repetitious passage, where the rhythm drowns out the sense: "I listen, and [...] I seek, like a caged beast born of caged beasts born of caged beasts born of caged beasts born in a cage and dead in a cage, born and then dead, born in a cage and then dead in a cage" (TN 386–87). Silence is also present in speech, in its interruptions: "The comma will come where I'll drown for good, then the silence (TN 409).

Silence inhabits speech: this is perhaps what is most scandalous about *The Unnamable*. The narrator is painfully aware that while we speak *with* words, words themselves do not speak; they are silent. We invest words with sense, but they have none on their own. Already Molloy had said, "All I know is what the words know" (TN 31), but what do words know? Very little. Thus the Unnamable speaks of "blank words," "dust of words," and calls words "drops of silence through the silence" (TN 408, 386, 382).

If the Unnamable manages to achieve silence in speech, he is also able to speak in the silence. As he says: "I'll speak of me when I speak no more" (TN 392); "I'd be the silence" (TN 413). We see how the Unnamable speaks in the silence as we read the last words in the text:

91

Perhaps they have carried me to the threshold of my story, before the door that opens on my story, that would surprise me, if it opens, it will be I, it will be the silence, where I am, I don't know, I'll never know, in the silence you don't know, you must go on, I can't go on, I'll go on.

Superficially the Unnamable's promise to go on speaking, followed by a silence, resembles Proust's ending to his seven-volume *Remembrance of Things Past*. The narrator, whose main concern has been his inability to write, declares at the end of the work that he will finally begin the work he has dreamt of. Judging from the description he provides of it, it will be quite like the text we have just read. The problem for us as readers then becomes: What have we been reading up to now? How can we read a work that has not yet been written? We must understand, paradoxically, that the book the narrator will now write is the idealized version of the one we have just read.

There is an important difference between Proust's and Beckett's use of the same strategy. Whereas Proust speaks of the absent text to follow as plenitude, Beckett announces his future work as silence: the Unnamable annexes silence as a text. Thus when Beckett has the Unnamable say "I'll go on" and then fall silent, he is not being coy or ironic. The Unnamable does go on speaking: in the silence, through the silence, *as* the silence.

The implications are astounding. Does this mean that whenever we come upon silence, we shall be reading *The Unnamable?* The text's project is not so grandiose. For in silence we read, we shall always read, and we always have read what we find in *The Unnamable:* not so much a book as "the pure approach to the movement whence all books come," as the critic Maurice Blanchot has written.[7] The Unnamable portrays the passage from silence to text, the desire to speak anew by silencing what has been said before: hence the Unnamable's subversion of the stories of "Mahood and Company."

Troublingly, the Unnamable shows us the transition from silence to literary creation by presenting an opposite movement: the passage from speech to silence. But his is a silence that is a literary creation in its own right. The Unnamable talks of the necessity to void the alter ego's voice that is "woven into" his own, but since all words are ultimately "others' words," he must fall silent in order to achieve his voice (TN 309, 386). However, so that he may appropriate the silence as his own, he must frame it by speech: the other's voice "will disappear one day, I hope, from mine, completely. But in order for that to happen I must speak, speak" (TN 309).

Beckett wrote *The Unnamable* in 1949, and after such an extreme literary experience it seems that he had to remain silent. Or rather, silence was actually part of his work. He did break his silence to translate his French works into English, to write his most famous plays, and to compose in 1950 *Textes pour rien (Texts for Nothing),* a series of prose pieces where we find, in abbreviated form, many of the same concerns voiced in *The Unnamable.* Beckett did not publish another novel until 1961, when he emerged with *Comment c'est* (translated as *How It Is*). The original French title is almost homonymous with the verb *commencer,* which means "to begin." By beginning to speak again in *How It Is,* Beckett frames the silence that started at the end of *The Unnamable.*

How It Is

Molloy's, Malone's, and the Unnamable's often endless sentences are actually easier to understand than the prose in this last full-length novel by Beckett. *How It Is* strings together short phrases into unpunctuated paragraphs, separated from each other by blank space. Let the first half-page serve as an example:

> how it was I quote before Pim with Pim after Pim how it is three parts I say it as I hear it

> voice once without quaqua on all sides then in me when the panting stops tell me again finish telling me invocation

> past moments old dreams back again or fresh like those that pass or things things always and memories I say them as I hear them murmur them in the mud

> in me that were without when the panting stops scraps of an ancient voice in me not mine

> my life last state last version ill-said ill-heard ill-recaptured ill-murmured in the mud brief movements of the lower face losses everywhere

The sonorous qualities, the rhythms of the repetitious words, are immediately perceptible; to appreciate the text on that level is already rewarding. As the narrator later says, "first the sound then the sense" (H 95). To grasp the sense of the lines above, typical of this novel as a whole, we must read phrase by phrase. This is not a specifically academic exercise; *How It Is* requires constant attentiveness to figure out what is going on at the most basic plot level. To proceed otherwise and give a linear summary of what happens would do great injustice to Beckett's challenge to the reader. Therefore, let us accompany him slowly through the novel's opening.

Paragraph 1

"how it was": The novel is called *How It Is;* why has the tense changed before we even begin? This riddle, like many others, is cleared up as we read on.

"I quote": The narrator immediately tells us that he is using someone else's words, an experience he shares with the Unnamable; the whole text has, as it were, quotation marks around it. Thus the last paragraph contains the words "end of quotation." Not only is the narrator here transmitting another's words; he later speaks of a witness who dictates his words to a scribe, who is writing down the version we read.

"before Pim with Pim after Pim": Here the narrator introduces a character named Pim. These three phrases reoccur throughout the book; many others do so as well; *How It Is* turns out to be the most repetitious of Beckett's works to date. Moreover, as elsewhere in Beckett, content restates form: later on in this paragraph we learn that "before Pim," "with Pim," and "after Pim" designate the "three parts" or chapters of the book, which recount the narrator's life before he met Pim, his existence with Pim, and the period after Pim has gone off.

"how it is": We have passed imperceptibly from "how it was" to "how it is." Does this mean that the narrator proposes to tell us how it *was* before he met Pim and while he was with Pim, and then he will tell us how it *is* now? The situation turns out to be more complicated than that. He will often use the present tense to narrate the past as well as the present situation, confusingly moving back and forth between them. This device plays upon the fact that in hearing a tale, we always experience it as a present, even when it is recounted in the past; fictional representation is always re-*present*-ation.

"three parts": Analyzed above.

"I say it as I hear it": This phrase is one of the most frequent refrains in the book. It occurs in modified form in the next paragraph: "I say them as I hear them." Even in its first occurrence this phrase is repetitious, in that it restates the earlier "I quote." The connotation, however, is different: "I say it as I hear it" implies that the narrator is plainspoken and that "it" (the story to be told) is communicated clearly enough to be reproduced. Such directness of expression and purpose stands in contrast to the Unnamable's tentativeness and interrogation of his own speech. Some critics have attributed this later definiteness in Beckett to the experience of writing for the theater, where the reality of the actors and stage is indisputable, even if the interpretation of events is entirely open. Later on, the narrator makes the theatrical import of *How It Is* explicit when he says, "the scene is empty," and "the curtains parted part one" (H 32, 53).

Paragraph 2

"voice once without quaqua on all sides then in me": This phrase describes how the narrator hears the voice that dictates to him; we must assume that the voice transmits to the hearer even the words describing how it sounds! There is a syntactically confusing element here, one of many in this text without punctuation: "without" has to be read as an adverb, not a preposition. The voice starts "without," that is, *outside* the narrator, surrounding him "on all sides"; "then" it moves inside him. "Quaqua" would suggest how the voice sounds; the voice is somehow imitating itself.

"when the panting stops": It seems that the narrator— or perhaps the voice, or both—pants; then the voice enters the narrator. "When the panting stops" is another refrain of the book. Perhaps the blocks of text separated by white space represent a kind of respiration: words come forth in rapid succession, causing panting; then silence falls, as the producer of the verbiage takes a breather.

"tell me again": The narrator here is asking the voice to tell him what to say; since he is repeating the voice's words, we have to imagine that the voice is telling him to ask itself what he should say. The "again" foreshadows how repetitious this text will be; it also suggests that the voice has been going on well before this text began. In a sense this voice is the agency that speaks through all of Beckett's narrators, the voice that investigated itself in *The Unnamable* but has now grown more sure of itself. Furthermore, if we view the trilogy and *How It Is* as forming a continuum, this would also be the voice that had spoken in the silence, as the silence, in the period that followed *The Unnamable.* Now it is speaking "again," as words.

"finish telling me": As in *The Unnamable,* the narrator wishes to fall silent; he must ask the inner voice, or the voice must ask itself, to stop speaking.

"invocation": This word designates a call for help, a supplication, such as worshipers make to God at the opening of prayer service; it is derived from the Latin word *vox,* meaning voice. The recursiveness is clear: like a dog biting its own tail, the narrator is voicing a plea to the inner voice that prompts his own voice. Moreover, the allusion to prayer in the word *invocation* is relevant in this text, which uses such rhythmic repetitions as occur in liturgy. Later in *How It Is* mention will be made of God ("curse God or bless him" [H 40]— as though the two were the same!) and of "prayer in vain [...] prayer for prayer's sake" (H 36). The theme of an inner voice reminds one of the voice of conscience, traditionally considered to be the voice of God. In *How It Is* that voice is devoid of moral considerations; it is only divine in that it creates a life, a story, for the hearer/narrator: "the voice quaqua from which I get my life" (H 113).

Paragraph 3

"past moments old dreams back again or fresh like those that pass or things things always and memories": These are some themes of which the voice will speak to the narrator and which he will reproduce for us: accounts of past moments; recurrent dreams dating back a long time; more recent ("fresh") dreams; things, in the sense of objects; finally memories, which are not necessarily the same as past moments. The latter may exist as mental images more than as intellectual remembrances.

"I say them as I hear them": Here this refrain refers to the moments, dreams, etc. of which the voice speaks.

"murmur them": The repetition becomes alliterative: "say the*m*," "hear the*m*," "*m*ur*m*ur the*m*." As seen in this phrase, and later in the narrator's and character's names (Pim and Bom), *How It Is* gives great importance to labials, the sounds formed with the lips, such as *p, m, b.* Later the narrator speaks of his "thirst for labials" (H 108), as though sounds were a physical substance that could be drunk.

"in the mud": This is the first reference to the narrator's present situation, lying in the mud, crawling like Molloy or Worm. Thus he speaks of existence before he met Pim as his "life in the light" (H 9 et passim), when presumably he walked upright and did not wallow.

Paragraph 4

"in me that were without": A modified repetition of the beginning of paragraph 2, now in the plural, referring to the voice telling of his past moments, dreams, etc.

"when the panting stops": This is a repetition of the refrain that first occurred in paragraph 2.

"scraps": The text consists only of phrases; this aspect is addressed here by one of the innumerable self-commentaries. The voice is said to speak (says it speaks) only in "scraps" (later on: "bits and scraps," "rags of life" [H 7, 21]). Scraps, bits, rags do not suggest pieces that can be reassembled into a whole, but rather inessential elements, residue; the phrases do not add up to full sentences but remain isolated. As the narrator describes it later, he speaks in "midget grammar": "sudden series subject object subject object quick succession and away" (H 76, 11). Totalization of the fragmented sentences, images, thoughts, is impossible in *How It Is;* there is no gaining a full understanding of the text because it is incomplete by its nature. What the German philosopher Theodor Adorno has said of *Endgame* is true of this work as well: to comprehend it is to comprehend its incomprehensibility.[8] Thus, as the narrator of *How It Is* speaks of a church banner, his words apply as well to his narrative: "here something illegible in the folds" (H 36). Likewise, he says that the sack Pim carries is "just one of those things that pass understanding there are some" (H 61).

"of an ancient voice in me not mine": Once again this refers to the otherness of the voice speaking outside and then inside the narrator. Now we learn that the voice is ancient, which again likens it to a divine voice. In *The Unnamable* the voice seemed eternal; likewise, the narrator in *How It Is* explains that by telling his tale in parts concerning the periods before, with, and after Pim, he will "divide into three a single eternity for the sake of clarity" (H 24).

Paragraph 5

"my life last state last version": This makes explicit that the narrator has existed before in other incarnations and that his story has been previously told. These earlier states and versions may well be the narrators in the trilogy and their diverse accounts.

"ill-said ill-heard ill-recaptured ill-murmured in the mud": Once again the focus is on the imperfect nature of the information being received and conveyed by the narrator. This formulation must have pleased Beckett, for he used it again in the title of a 1981 prose piece, *Ill Seen Ill Said*. The repetition of the word *ill* is to be savored in Beckett's pessimistic universe; in the French original the insistence on the word *mal* adds a labial element: "mal dite mal entendue mal retrouvée mal murmurée." The concern with imperfect communication and wording is voiced in another oft-repeated self-commentary in *How It Is:* "something wrong there" (H 10, 16 et passim).

"brief movements of the lower face" refer perhaps to talking, especially in such short phrasing as one finds in *How It Is*. Note the labials (*brief movements*), especially in the French original: "*brefs mouvements du bas du visage pertes partout.*"

"losses everywhere": It is a tenet of physics that the universe is tending toward ever greater entropy, that is, loss of order. *How It Is* depicts the increasing disorganization of information: the message gets presumably more jumbled as it goes from voice to teller to witness to scribe to reader; what one hears as "aha" might signify "mamma" (H 26). The book also shows entropy in the evolutionary sphere as the narrator, who speaks of a "loss of species" (H 27; cf. H 47), regresses from the more highly specialized order of the bipeds to the less complex crawling animals who live in the "warmth of the primeval mud impenetrable dark" (H 11).

In these opening passages, as in the rest of the book, the narrator jumps from one concern to the next. For example, paragraphs 2, 3, and 4 speak first of the voice, then of panting, then of elements of a more traditional story (the past, dreams, objects, memories), then of murmuring the words conveying these plot elements; after that, existence in the mud is mentioned, and then we return to considerations of voice and of panting. To keep matters somewhat straight, we have to read slowly, moving no faster than the narrator of *How It Is* through the mud: "I crawl in an amble ten yards fifteen yards halt"; "at the speed of thirty-seven or thirty-eight say forty yards a year we advance" (H 19, 125). Yet working at it long enough, we can arrive somewhere: we could complete "in eight thousand years [...] the girdle of the earth" (H 41). Many commentators go through the book much faster, focusing on its most recognizably anecdotal element, the narrator's relationship with Pim, though in the first part it is only alluded to in passing. These critics downplay the images there that impinge intermittently on the narrator's consciousness, reminding him of his life before he crawled in the mud.

The first picture that occurs to him recalls Molloy watching the meeting of A and C: "some creature or other I watched him after my fashion from afar through my spyglass" (H 9). What next appears is more unsavory: "I pissed and shat another image in my crib never so clean since" (H 9). This wallowing in dirt foreshadows the narrator's life in the mud. Insofar as in psychoanalytic theory excrement functions as a part-object (a fragment of the body that captivates the subject, to whom it appears as a whole unto itself[9]), these bodily wastes are not unrelated to the isolated objects that the narrator finds in his possession as he crawls: a rope, a sack, tins ("cans," in American parlance) of fish, and a tin-opener. These objects obviously come in pairs (the sack is tied by the rope, the tins are opened by the opener), but like psychoanalytic part-objects their origin is obscured: "the sack whence the sack"; "the tin-opener there's another object"; "the cord from the sack there's another object"; "a celestial tin miraculous sardines sent down by God" (H 7, 9, 11, 48).

Even words and sounds function as objects in the psychoanalytic sense. We have seen how the narrator has a thirst for labial consonants, as though mother's milk consisted of *m*'s; likewise, in a love scene remembered from his sixteenth year he and his girlfriend feed on terms of endearment as well as sandwiches: "my sweet girl I bite she swallows my sweet boy she bites I swallow [...] my darling girl I bite she swallows my darling boy she bites I swallow" (H 30–31). There is also a fetishistic indulgence in rare words that stand out in the otherwise drab vocabulary; the critic Susan Brienza has drawn up a list of these: prepensely, speluncar, deasil, apostil, halm, oakum, iso, dextogyre, sinistro.[10]

Such words attest to the narrator's extensive knowledge: he claims he "always understood everything except for example history and geography" (H 41). Even here entropy encroaches, for at one time his knowledge had been more complete. Thus he misses "the humanities I had," "the geography I had"; "I've lost my latin" (H 42). His residual learning serves strange purposes, as when he compares two symmetrical parts of his body: "one buttock twice too big the other twice too small [...] in other words the ratio four to one I always loved arithmetic it has paid me back in full" (H 37). This reminds us once again of Molloy, who exclaimed upon calculating the number of farts he emitted per day, "Extraordinary how mathematics help you to know yourself" (TN 30). Likewise, the narrator's memory of love at sixteen has an anal dimension; he sees himself with the girl "whom I hold who holds me by the hand the arse I have" (H 29). Taking into account the Freudian relationship between odor and anality, we should note that the girl has a dog that "lowers its snout to its black and pink penis too tired to lick it" (H 30). Throughout his oeuvre Beckett makes us experience a terrible authenticity in exposing the attraction such abject details exert upon us; for example, Moran says of his neighbor's dog: "I could see his little black penis ending in a thin wisp of wetted hair" (TN 105). Beckett also depicts faithfully the way we chase such concerns from our awareness: "smaller and smaller out of sight first the dog then us the scene is shut of us" (H 31). The image that follows this one, of some sheep and a horse in the country, is also brutally pushed out of consciousness: "it's over it's done I've had the image" (H 31).

Contrarily to James Joyce, whose stream-of-consciousness technique reflects the belief that we engage in constant interior monologue, Beckett in *How It Is* might have gotten far closer to the reality of our thought processes, which are characterized not only by flow but also by gaps. Thus it might be the careful imitation of thought that makes this text so difficult. When we read a traditional novel where the plot thickens step by step, we can switch our attention "on and off" (H 8), and enough information will pass through for us to follow the story. But lest we miss a basic element of *How It Is,* whose prose is as intermittent as our usual manner of attention, we have to synchronize ourselves with the text's ebb and flow: we have to "time the voice [... and] time the silence that might help" (H 40). Otherwise there will be "so many words so many lost one every three two every five" (H 95). (The meticulous attempt to portray thought processes may be what allows Beckett to use the seemingly presumptuous title *How It Is,* as though the book were the definitive word on some aspect of life.)

Communication is a problem posed time and again in this book, especially in part 2, which addresses the central concern: "life with Pim." The narrator encounters a fellow creature crawling in the mud, with whom he performs gyrations, like reptiles copulating in shallow waters: remember that Malone said his alter ego Macmann was "more reptile than bird" (TN 243). Similar to Molloy unsure of his love Lousse's sex, the narrator of *How It Is* does not know whether he has met "man woman girl or boy," but upon groping "a testicle or two" and a bald skull, he realizes the other is "a little old man we're two little old men" (H 54): we are in the presence of the Beckettian pseudocouple. The narrator's interest in this individual is heightened when he hears him singing a little tune, but like the reader of *How It Is* he comes across words that at first make no sense to him: "I can't make out the words the mud muffles or perhaps a foreign tongue" (H 56). Faced with this incomprehensible and uncomprehending creature, the narrator digs his fingernails deeply into Pim's armpit to demand that he continue to sing. He works up an entire system of such signs: a thump on the skull tells Pim to sing, the blade of the can opener plunged into Pim's buttocks means he should speak, the handle of the can opener plunged into the kidney signifies he should sing or speak louder, the index finger introduced into Pim's anus orders him to sing or speak more softly, a clap across the buttocks means "bravo" (H 69).

As though this system were not complicated enough, another confusing element is introduced. The narrator merges his own words with Pim's, as he notes (without quotation marks, in typically Beckettian style) what Pim "must have said to himself" as the blows are inflicted: "what is required of me now what is the meaning of this new torment" (H 67). Again the parallel with the reader's predicament is clear: what is the meaning of this new tormented prose that Beckett is inflicting upon us?

The torture becomes ever greater, for the narrator adds to his communication with Pim a writing system: with his nails he carves words into Pim's back, bloodying it. This procedure led the American novelist John Updike to compare *How It Is* to Kafka's *The Penal Colony,* where a prisoner's sentence is etched by a terrible machine onto his back, so that he would internalize it in the most literal sense.[11] Such forms of writing are not inventions of the twentieth-century literary mind, but are literary reworkings of ancient practices of bodily inscription: tatooing, scarification, caste markings, circumcision.

It is through such writing that the narrator gives his fellow creature the name of Pim. He carves "YOU PIM pause YOU PIM in the furrows" (H 71). As he names Pim, so he concocts a story for him, as Malone did for Sapo/Macmann: "samples my life above [that is, in the light, before crawling in the mud] Pim's life we're talking of Pim my life up there my wife" (H 76). Here we see the narrator putting words into Pim's mouth ("my life above," "my life up there," "my wife"), identifying himself with the other to the point of claiming his name is also Pim! Realizing the confusion this could bring about, he says that Pim should call him Bom and carves that name onto his buttocks: "BOM scored by finger-nail athwart the arse the vowel in the hole" (H 60). Once again we may appreciate how serious Beckett was when he said his work is "a matter of fundamental sounds": the *o* is literally the "fundament," a word that signifies "anus."[12]

A Beckettian habit has changed: the *m,* which began the characters' names in earlier works, ends them here: Pim, Bom, Pam Prim (Pim's wife), Kram and

Krim (the witness and scribe who record what is happening in *How It Is*), and Skom Skum (the dog who licks the speaker's genitals). The narrator addresses this naming strategy directly: "m at the end and one syllable the rest indifferent" (H 60).

The reversal of the name (the initial becomes the terminal letter) partakes of the terrible recursiveness of this book, whose narrator constantly speaks of the production of his own speech and where the past is narrated as an eternally returning present. Thus the Bom-Pim story repeats itself after their separation, for part 3 anticipates a fourth part—never written—where the narrator Bom would play the tortured Pim's role to a torturer like himself; hence we understand why Bom originally said his name was Pim too. Part 5— were it to be written—would recount the period after Bom has left his torturer and is moving toward his victim, Pim; part 6 would recount, as part 2, Bom's life with Pim. The process would go on endlessly: "think of the couple we were Pim and I part two and shall be again part six ten fourteen so on" (H 121).

But just as the book is infinitely extendible in the future, so it is in the past; there is no assurance that part 1 was actually the beginning, for with every occurrence of the cycle victim and torturer believe it is the first time: "when on the unpredictable arse for the millionth time the groping hand descends [...] for the hand it is the first arse for the arse the first hand" (H 121). Freud had told us the same: every time we form a relationship we may well have the impression we have found a new love, but we are unconsciously repeating an earlier one. "The finding of an object is in fact a refinding of it."[13]

If the Bom-Pim relationship is endlessly extendible in time, so it is in space: the narrator is not the
only one to move between victim and torturer; in turn,
these two do the same, and so do *their* victims and
torturers, ad infinitum. That is to say, while Bom is
torturing Pim, Bom's tormentor is being tortured by
another creature; then, while Bom is being tortured,
Pim is torturing another creature. As each torture ses-
sion is finished, the former torturer moves to the one
who will torture him, and the former victim moves to
the creature whom he will torment—and then back
again.

Thus *How It Is* presents an entire world made up
of a long series of torturers and victims. So that each
creature may have both a torturer and a victim, they
must be either infinite in number or finite but in circular formation:

> as for example our course a closed curve and let us
> be numbered 1 to 1000000 then number 1000000 on
> leaving his tormentor number 999999 instead of launch-
> ing forth into the wilderness towards an inexistent
> victim proceeds towards number 1 (н 117).

Likewise, if there were fifty million beings, those numbered 1 and 50,000,000 would form a couple with each
other, as well as with numbers 2 and 49,999,999 respectively, so that everyone in the series would have two
neighbors: his tormentor and his victim.

The complicated numbering system reflects the fascination with mathematics that had already emerged
in the permutations of *Watt* and in the pebble-sucking
and farting scenes in *Molloy;* far less humorously, it is
reminiscent of the penchant of totalitarians for num-

109

bering those who live under them. This extreme mathematical meticulousness demonstrates how the classical art of recounting a story degenerates, in a dehumanized world, into a kind of counting.

The tone is hypothetical in part 3, which offers different possible figures for how many torturers and victims there are in all, and then even conceives of a world in which there would be "never any Pim never any Bom never any journey never anything but the dark" (H 127). Despite the title, *How It Is* admits presenting things not as they are or were (allowing for the present to function as a historical past), but only as they could be or could have been:

  all these calculations yes explanations yes the whole
  story from beginning to end yes completely false yes

  that wasn't how it was no not at all no how then no
  answer how was it then no answer (H 144).

Thus the third part undermines the apparent definiteness of *How It Is;* the story it tells turns out to be as tentative as the ones recounted in *The Unnamable.*

However, an important difference remains between the two texts. Whereas the Unnamable rejects stories and words as inevitably belonging to others so that he has no choice but to annex silence as his own voice, the narrator of *How It Is* comes to accept the voice that prompts him as his own. He dismisses as "all balls"—just so much nonsense—"all this business of voices [. . .] of someone in another world [. . .] whose kind of dream I am" (H 145). Rather, he discovers that

110

I have a voice yes in me yes (H 145)

yes my voice yes mine yes not another's no mine
alone yes sure yes when the panting stops yes on and
off yes a few words yes a few scraps yes that no one
hears not but less and less no answers LESS AND
LESS yes (H 146).

This "yes" has a literary antecedent: it occurs in
Molly Bloom's monologue at the end of James Joyce's
Ulysses: "first I put my arms around him yes and drew
him down to me so he could feel my breasts all perfume
yes and his heart was going like mad and yes I said yes
I will Yes." But whereas in Joyce the "yes" asserts the
fullness of the perceived world, in Beckett's text "yes"
underlines the sheer perceiving of an ever emptier world,
made up of "LESS AND LESS." Moreover, *How It Is*
ends by annihilating not only the world as perceived
or invented but also the agency that perceives or invents that world, by killing off the *I:*

DIE screams I MAY DIE screams I SHALL DIE screams
good

good good end at last of part three and last that's
how it was end of quotation after Pim how it is (H
147).

As in *Malone Dies* the narrator here attempts to
approach the impossible utterance *I die.* But who speaks
the last words, those which take the place of *I die:*
"good good end at last [. . .] end of quotation after Pim
how it is"? Can the *I* effect such closure of his own
discourse? Is he like the Unnamable, annexing silence

111

in order to tell us "how it is," how "it"—be it silence or death—is? Or rather, could this be, once again, the agency who the narrator said at the beginning of the book was dictating to him, and whom he declares no longer existent toward the end of the book? Perhaps when the narrator said to us that no outer voice existed, he was simply quoting the outer voice? The apparent definiteness of this book reveals itself as indeterminacy. The title *How It Is* must be understood ironically.

NOTES

1. Jean Blanzat, quoted on the back cover of *Molloy,* Editions de Minuit, Collection "Double"; my translation.

2. Hugh Kenner, "The Cartesian Centaur," *Samuel Beckett: A Critical Study*, new rev. ed. (Berkeley: University of California Press, 1968) 117–32.

3. Ludovic Janvier, *Pour Samuel Beckett* (Paris: Editions de Minuit, 1966) 52.

4. Georges Bataille, "Molloy's Silence," *On Beckett: Essays and Criticism,* ed. S. E. Gontarski (New York: Grove, 1986) 138.

5. Jacques Derrida, *Speech and Phenomenon* (Evanston: Northwestern University Press, 1973) 96.

6. Elmar Tophoven kindly pointed out this passage from Grillparzer's *Des Meeres und der Liebe Wellen,* 1. 2068.

7. Maurice Blanchot, "Where Now? Who Now?" Gontarski 144. I have modified the translation somewhat to conform more closely to the original.

8. Theodor Adorno, "Towards an Understanding of *Endgame,*" trans. Samuel M. Weber, *Twentieth Century Interpretations of* Endgame, ed. Bell Gale Chevigny (Englewood Cliffs, NJ: Prentice-Hall, 1969) 84.

9. See the entry "Part-Object," *The Language of Psycho-analysis,* Jean Laplanche and J.-B. Pontalis, trans. Donald Nicholson-Smith (New York: Norton, 1973) 301–02.

10. Susan Brienza, *Samuel Beckett's New Worlds* (Norman: University of Oklahoma Press, 1987) 93–94.

11. "John Updike in 'New Yorker,'" *Samuel Beckett: The Critical Heritage,* ed. Lawrence Graver and Raymond Federman (London: Routledge and Kegan Paul, 1979) 257.

12. "Beckett's Letters on *Endgame,*" *Village Voice* 19 Mar. 1958: 15.

13. Freud, *Three Essays on the Theory of Sexuality, Standard Edition* 7: 222.

CHAPTER FOUR

Major Theatrical Works (1948–61)

Waiting for Godot

Beckett's play *En attendant Godot (Waiting for Godot)*, written in 1948 and first performed in 1953, has become well known to the point of having spawned the graffiti "Back in five minutes—Godot," referring ironically to the nonappearance of the personage awaited so faithfully by the two protagonists, Vladimir and Estragon. As the play opens, we find these two hoboes, who call each other affectionately Didi and Gogo, on a country road bare except for a leafless tree. There they remain, waiting for Godot, for the two acts of the play, perhaps representing two consecutive days. Some interruptions occur: in the middle of each act there appears a landed gentleman called Pozzo, accompanied by his carrier, ironically named Lucky, whom he keeps attached by means of a rope; and at the end of each act a boy arrives who claims to be sent by Godot. Curiously, he calls Vladimir "Mister Albert" and informs him each time that Godot will not be coming today, but that he will surely be there tomorrow.

To while away the time Vladimir and Estragon exchange words regarding discomforts of their bodies and clothing, episodes of their some fifty years together, and questions of theology. Except for an occasional longer discourse by Vladimir, the more philosophical of the two, they speak to each other in extremely short phrases, as though they knew each other's thoughts so well as to need only to refer to things in the barest of terms. The result is quick dialogue, sometimes lapsing into vaudeville routine, as when they mirror other's obsequious courteousness and then, just as mechanically, each other's hostility:

Vladimir and Estragon (turning simultaneously): Do you—

Vladimir:	Oh, pardon!
Estragon:	Carry on.
Vladimir:	No no, after you.
Estragon:	No no, you first.
Vladimir:	I interrupted you.
Estragon:	On the contrary.

They glare at each other angrily.

Vladimir:	Ceremonious ape!
Estragon:	Punctilious pig! (wFG 48)

Didi and Gogo then decide it would be a good diversion to hurl insults at one another. They try "Moron!", "Vermin!", and "Sewer-rat!", but the epithet that brings this shouting match to a close is "Crritic!" *(sic),* as though no worse term of abuse could be imagined (wFG 48). Warning enough for all those who attempt to judge this play; notwithstanding, it is one of the most commented-upon works of our time.

Beckett's preeminence as a playwright is all the

more surprising, as he had no theatrical training. One might imagine that a novelist turning to the theater would concentrate on its most novelistic aspect—story line or plot—but Beckett has always taken an extreme interest in production, providing copious stage directions and even directing several performances of his own plays. Actually this is not inconsistent with his novels, which are less concerned with telling stories than presenting narrative voice. These works seem already composed in a theatrical genre, the monologue; in fact, sections of the trilogy have been performed on stage.[1]

In addition, Beckett's early novel *Mercier and Camier* is even more evidently theatrical, containing long passages of quick dialogue between the title characters. Mercier and Camier constitute Beckett's first fully formed pseudocouple (a term discussed in chapter 1 above). In the history of the pseudocouple, the complimentarity between its members has often been symbolized by their physical form. One—usually the more intelligent or worldly, or higher in social standing—is tall and thin (think of Don Quixote, or Bouvard in Flaubert's *Bouvard and Pécuchet*), while the other (Sancho Panza, Pécuchet) is short and plump. *In Waiting for Godot* these roles fall respectively to Vladimir and Estragon, who are like the pseudocouple Laurel and Hardy—as well as another hobo/clown prototype, Charlie Chaplin—in another way: they wear bowler hats.

How the pseudocouple functions in *Godot* is clear from this dialogue where Vladimir and Estragon speak of the "prayer" or "supplication" they claim once to have presented to Godot:

116

Estragon:	And what did he reply?
Vladimir:	That he'd see.
Estragon:	That he couldn't promise anything.
Vladimir:	That he'd have to think it over.
Estragon:	In the quiet of his home.
Vladimir:	Consult his family.
Estragon:	His friends.
Vladimir:	His agents.
Estragon:	His correspondents.
Vladimir:	His books.
Estragon:	His bank account.
Vladimir:	Before taking a decision. (wfg 13)

The similarity between Didi's and Gogo's lines is clear: both use short phrases that do little more than further a larger sentence answering Estragon's original question; it is as though each were unable to complete a sentence, or even a thought, on his own. Yet there is an important difference between the two: Vladimir is the one who starts answering the question; it is he who knows more. At various points he must remind Estragon, who tends to forget such things, why they are not leaving the place they happen to be. "We are waiting for Godot," Vladimir says repeatedly, thus turning the title of the play into a refrain.

The rapid and repetitious give-and-take between Didi and Gogo can be quite funny in performance. It is just one case of Beckett's exploitation of the humor inherent in the reduction of human beings to machines.

117

This technique is used as well at the beginning of *Mercier and Camier,* where the two protagonists fail to rendezvous at a preordained place. Each repeatedly arrives there, waits for the other, and then leaves to search for him just before the other arrives. So machinelike are their actions that the narrator presents them in a chart that resembles a railroad schedule (MC 9):

		Arr.	*Dep.*	*Arr.*	*Dep.*	*Arr.*	*Dep.*	*Arr.*
Mercier	.	9.05	9.10	9.25	9.30	9.40	9.45	9.50
Camier	.	9.15	9.20	9.35	9.40	9.50		

This passage is comical in a theatrical way; the device of the chart makes it clear how much more visual than narrative the joke is. Routines that derive humor from mechanistic repetition are used time and again in *Waiting for Godot.* On one occasion Didi and Gogo briskly pass back and forth three hats between them, so that at any point each has one hat while the third is traveling between them. In another sequence Vladimir looks through his pockets for a radish but repeatedly takes out turnips. The play ends on a gag as well, as the two characters debate whether to hang themselves. Lacking rope, they decide to try a belt. Estragon removes his, and his pants fall down.

The contrast between the pathos of the characters driven to suicide and the bathos of the dropping pants is emblematic of the dual nature of *Waiting for Godot.* In one of its first reviews the French dramatist Jean Anouilh described the play as "Pascal's *Pensées* performed by the Fratellini clowns."[2] By coupling the pessimistic writings of the seventeenth-century philoso-

118

pher with a circus act, Anouilh shows how *Waiting for Godot* combines meditations on the meaninglessness of existence with the most frivolous distractions. Yet in no way does the copresence of these opposite modes mitigate the effect of each; rather, each comes to participate in the other. The meaninglessness of life is so grave as to require that we divert our attention from it; our diversions are so frivolous that they only deepen our awareness of life's meaninglessness. If Beckett calls *Waiting for Godot* a "tragicomedy," this is not to imply that it is a tragedy with some comic elements or a comedy with tragic ones. It is at once both comedy and tragedy, with the contradiction between them apparent but reconciled.

The dual nature of the play is observable in the ambiguity surrounding the figure of Godot. He sometimes seems to be no more than a powerful, though human, personage from whom Didi and Gogo need to ask a favor, as when they imagine Godot consulting his family, friends, agents, etc. to answer their request. Yet from Kafka's world—reflected in Moran's tale in the second half of Beckett's *Molloy*—we have learned that human bureaucracies in their arbitrariness symbolize God's inexplicable workings. Thus Godot looms as a divine figure, Didi and Gogo's fruitless wait represents humanity's desire for a message from a God fallen silent, and the boy sent by Godot appears as a Christ figure, God's innocent emissary.

An important Christian reference occurs within the first few minutes of the play, when Vladimir remarks, "One of the thieves was saved" (WFG 8). This is a reference to the Gospel according to Luke (23:43), who recounts that of the two men who were crucified

119

along with Jesus, one was sent to heaven, and the other to hell. This is a favorite story of Beckett's, which he alluded to as well in *Murphy,* in *Malone Dies,* and in an interview:

> I am interested in the shape of ideas even if I do not believe in them. There is a wonderful sentence in Augustine.... "Do not despair; one of the thieves was saved. Do not presume; one of the thieves was damned." That sentence has a wonderful shape. It is the shape that matters.[3]

Despite Beckett's formalist view of this quotation its theological significance is powerful. Grace is inexplicable: the two thieves were guilty of the same crime but their souls had different fates. The apparent arbitrariness of God's workings is suggested as well in Vladimir's discussion with the boy, who recounts that his brother, who tends sheep, is beaten by Godot, while he, a goatherd, is spared. This reminds us of the first brothers, the sons of Adam: Abel, whose sacrifice God accepts, is murdered by Cain, whose offering God refuses. This legend shows up elsewhere in *Godot:* Estragon addresses Pozzo and Lucky as Abel and Cain, remarking of the latter, "He's all humanity" (wfg 54). Our heroes' calling their request to Godot a "kind of prayer," a "vague supplication," enhances the theological texture (wfg 13). The French original has an additional resonance: in English Pozzo says he is taking Lucky to be sold at "the fair" (wfg 21), but in French they are going to the "marché de Saint-Sauveur," literally *the Holy Savior's market.*

Yet Beckett does much to undercut the theological substance. Emblematic in this regard is the name "Godot," which appends to the word *God* the playful French suffix -*ot*. Likewise, after mentioning one thief's salvation and the other's damnation, Vladimir says, "It's a reasonable percentage" (WFG 8), a remark that smacks of practical realism in a sphere supposedly devoid of such considerations. Pascal had also employed such reasoning in his bold theological "wager." He postulated that we should hedge our bets by worshiping God even if we do not believe in him, just in case he should turn out to exist. The recourse to bookkeeping by the philosopher no less than the clownish tramp shows how helpless we are with respect to God's silence. Similarly an exchange between Estragon and Vladimir that parodies the dogma of the imitation of Christ also underscores its pathos. Much comic effect is achieved in the play through Estragon's endless complaining about his boots, and on one occasion he declares he will go barefoot, as "Christ did" (WFG 34). Vladimir pushes Estragon's purely superficial identification with the Messiah a bit further by pointing out that "where he lived it was warm." "Yes," replies Estragon, "and they crucified quick" (WFG 34). This one-liner certainly makes the central event of Jesus' life ridiculous by reducing crucifixion to an assembly-line activity, but it derives its force from the unseemly but therefore vivid way it reveals to us Jesus' suffering.

We cannot be sure how to interpret the religious allusion surrounding Godot, and Beckett himself was of little help. He said that if he knew who Godot was, he would have said so in the play, and his characters share in the ignorance. Thus Estragon and Vladimir, sighting Pozzo in act 1, wonder if he is Godot. After Pozzo gives his name, pronounced "Po'dzo," Vladimir, who does not need to be told things twice, informs Estragon that this man is definitely not the one they are waiting for. But Estragon mishears the name Pozzo as "Godot," and then "Bozzo." A vaudevillesque routine ensues, wherein the two protagonists quizzically repeat "Pozzo" and "Bozzo," and Vladimir even says "Gozzo," while Pozzo is forced to explode his name "PPPOZZZO" (WFG 15). Once again we see how incisive Beckett's judgment was when he said his work is "a matter of fundamental sounds." This is true as well of the nicknames Didi and Gogo, which some critics interpret with respect to the simplest of words. Vladimir/Didi, the more articulate and masterful of the two, tells (French *dit,* pronounced "dee") Estragon/Gogo where to *go*— Estragon, who has such trouble going anywhere because of his bad shoes! Even the title and refrain *Waiting for Godot,* with its three *o* sounds ("waiting for Godot"), is repetitious; it is even more so in the original French, where the title *En attendant Godot* and the refrain "On attend Godot" are made up of a series of nasal and nonnasal *a* and *o* sounds: /ānatādāgodo/, /ōnatāgodo/.

Within this repetitiousness the visit of Pozzo and Lucky provides great distraction, for Didi and Gogo as well as the spectator. Our heroes are most fascinated by the slave. They examine the running sore on his neck, caused by the chafing of the rope that binds him to Pozzo; they ask what the baggage he carries contains, and why he does not put it down when he stops walking. The answer to the first question is "Sand," reminding us of how purposeless human toil is (WFG 57). Responding to the second question requires long gestural and rhetorical preliminaries on Pozzo's part.

He repeatedly sprays his throat, bombastically restates the question, and finally answers that Lucky holds the baggage needlessly in order to impress him. Despite the fuss, all soon forget that the question was posed and answered, and it is asked again. But by then Lucky has put down the baggage; hence the question is no longer relevant—or as Vladimir more strongly and falsely puts it: "Since he has put down his bags it is impossible we should have asked why he does not do so" (WFG 27). It is as though the only thing that mattered were the present situation, made ever more weighty by the endless wait for Godot.

This forgetfulness allows Vladimir to be completely ignorant of Pozzo's and Lucky's identity when they arrive on the scene and to remark after they have gone, "How they've changed" (WFG 32), implying he had met them before. Of course, Estragon is forgetful to the point of needing to be reminded several times that they are waiting for Godot. Likewise, Pozzo, upon returning in the second act, insists he has never passed that way before.

When he reappears, Pozzo's unawareness is figured symbolically, for he has lost his sight. A remark of his makes it unclear whether the two acts represent two consecutive days: he claims he "woke up one fine day as blind as Fortune," and he dismisses Vladimir's objection that "no later than yesterday" he could still see (WFG 55). Ambiguity remains, however, for Pozzo adds that "the blind have no notion of time." In this respect Vladimir and Estragon are blind as well. They speak of what occurred in act 1 as if it happened the day before, although between its end and the beginning of act 2 enough time has passed for leaves to have sprouted on the previously barren tree., All time has collapsed into three days: the entire past is conflated into *yesterday,* when Godot could have come but did not; the present is *today,* when Godot could come at any second; and the future is *tomorrow,* when (as the characters tell themselves) Godot will most surely come, if he fails to do so today.

The feeling dawns upon us that Vladimir and Estragon are willfully blind to the fact that they shall be forever waiting for Godot. In this sense Vladimir once again emerges as the more lucid. When the boy claiming to be sent by Godot comes on stage in the second act, asserting he had not been there before and promising— as he had done previously—that Godot would come the next day, Vladimir has an inkling of how repetitious this all is. He says, "Off we go again" (WFG 58).

Complementing the other characters' blindness is Lucky's attitude, impassive to the point of muteness. There are exceptions: when Pozzo perversely urges Estragon to express his caring to the slave, the pitiable one delivers a swift kick to his would-be benefactor. Thereupon Vladimir's and Estragon's sympathies shift to Pozzo; so much for the steadfastness of human kindness. However, Lucky is best remembered by most theatergoers for his three-page monologue. Vladimir and Estragon are incredulous when Pozzo informs them that he has learned all he knows from his dumb slave, so the master gives the order "Think!" What then spews forth from Lucky's mouth begins thus:

> Given the existence as uttered forth in the public works of Puncher and Wattmann of a personal God quaquaquaqua with white beard quaquaquaqua out-

124

side time without extension who from the heights of divine apathia divine athambia divine aphasia loves us dearly with some exceptions for reasons unknown (WFG 28).

Lucky soon leaves the theological realm to go on wildly about topics drawn from psychology, physiology, philosophy, geography, etc. It would be unwarranted to extract a conclusive message from such incoherent speech that reduces scholarly thought to drivel, but in accordance with Beckett's fascination with the "shape of ideas" there is something well formed about Lucky's Godot-like personal though inaccessible God, placed at "the heights of divine apathia divine athambia divine aphasia." *Apathia* means lack of feeling, *athambia* means imperturbability and *aphasia* means lack of speech. Lucky is saying that in his self-sufficiency God need not feel for man, or be disturbed by him, or speak to him. However, the scientific terms *apathia, athambia,* and *aphasia* do not describe divine attributes but rather the state of psychotics out of touch with the world. God would be mad, according to the generally aphasiac but now raving lunatic that Lucky is.

Moreover, the experts whom Lucky cites as the guarantors of the existence of God, Puncher and Wattmann, remind us of Beckett's mad character Watt, and not only because of the similarity in name. We first caught sight of Watt at a streetcar stop, and "wattman" is a word that the French believe is English for a streetcar driver; "puncher," in turn, would refer to the conductor who cancels the passengers' tickets. Thus the "public works of Wattman and Puncher" refer less to the published works of two scholars than to a system of public transportation. Lucky's ravings about God, as out of control as a cableless streetcar going downhill, actually are about streetcars. His rantings about other sciences similarly displace their supposed object. For example, anthropometry, the study of the measurement and proportions of the human body, is overlain with excrement when Lucky speaks of its being pursued at the "Acacacacademy of Anthropopopometry": *caca* and *popo* are French baby terms for feces and chamberpot.

In reading the play we can study Lucky's speech at leisure, but in seeing a production we are struck most of all by the uninterrupted rapidity with which it pours forth, and by the superbly comic detail that ends it. Vladimir and Estragon, driven to distraction by Lucky's ravings, pounce upon him to no avail. Pozzo lets them in on the sole means of silencing his slave: removing his hat. As soon as they do so, he stops midstream, ironically enough on the word "unfinished" (WFG 29). It is as though all his learning were not only terribly jumbled but the brain that houses it detachable as well.

When Vladimir and Estragon perform their vaudeville number with the three hats, their placement of Lucky's bowler on their own heads corresponds to their identification with him. Like the slave dependent on Pozzo for sustenance, our heroes' existence is defined by Godot: as Lucky is attached to his master by a rope, so Estragon wonders whether Vladimir and he are "tied" to Godot (WFG 14). Hence their fascination with Lucky's running scores and commiseration with his purposeless tasks, the symbols of their own dereliction. No help, only bondage, is to be expected from the present Pozzo and the absent Godot.

On another level the attachment between Pozzo and Lucky literalizes the master-slave relationship between our heroes. As Lucky is beaten by Pozzo, Estragon is wounded emotionally by Vladimir, who often turns a deaf ear to his requests for attention and tenderness. Pozzo knows that Lucky is dependent on him for sustenance; likewise, Vladimir remarks to Estragon, "But for me ... where would you be ... You'd be nothing more than a little heap of bones at the present minute" (wfg 7).

Moreover, like Pozzo, who sprays his throat to enhance his speech while his slave remains mute, Vladimir has a gift for rhetorical flourish while Estragon speaks plainly. Thus Estragon concentrates on putting on and taking off his shoes, whereas Vladimir remarks sententiously: "There's man all over for you, blaming on his boots the faults of his feet" (wfg 8). Estragon simply asks why Lucky does not put his bags down, but Vladimir judges that "it's a scandal" to treat Lucky so cruelly (wfg 18). The difference between the lofty-minded Vladimir and the physically obsessed Estragon make comparisons of this pseudocouple to Don Quixote and Sancho Panza particularly apt. Thus when Estragon, prey to his bodily needs, falls asleep, Vladimir goes off on a philosophical disquisition about a spiritual kind of sleep:

Was I sleeping, while the others suffered? Am I sleeping now? To-morrow, when I wake, or think I do, what shall I say of to-day? [...] *(He looks again at Estragon.)* At me too someone is looking, of me too someone is saying, He is sleeping, he knows nothing, let him sleep on. *(Pause.)* I can't go on! *(Pause.)* What have I said? (wfg 58).

127

The end of this speech, when Vladimir says "I can't go on" and then speaks more, foreshadows the final words of *The Unnamable:* "I can't go on, I'll go on." However, the question of whether one's life is spent asleep to Truth, of whether existence is real or imaginary, proceeds from a classical debate. The sixteenth-century Spanish dramatist Pedro Calderón de la Barca expressed it succinctly in the title of his tragedy, *La vida es sueño* (*Life Is a Dream*), lines from which Beckett quotes in his monograph on Proust (P 49): "Pues el delito mayor/ Del hombre es haber nacido" *(For man's greatest crime is to have been born)*. Beckett incorporates this idea into an exchange between Vladimir and Estragon:

Vladimir:	Suppose we repented.
Estragon:	Repented what?
Vladimir:	Oh . . . *(He reflects.)* We wouldn't have to go into the details.
Estragon:	Our being born? (WFG 8)

Here Estragon waxes as sententious as Vladimir; in a stage direction elsewhere Beckett writes that Estragon becomes "aphoristic for once" (WFG 51). Conversely, there are moments when Vladimir acts like his sidekick. Despite his spirituality, he experiences at least one pressing bodily need à la Gogo and runs offstage to urinate; on another occasion, his diffidence notwithstanding, he is panic-stricken when the usually submissive Gogo abandons him to go into the wings. Vladimir's greater lucidity, however, allows him to rec-

128

ognize that sometimes Estragon is in the position of power: in suggesting that they play at being Pozzo and Lucky, Vladimir asks for the slave's part. But neither are Pozzo's and Lucky's roles rigorously separate. When Pozzo comes blind onto the stage, it is clear he needs Lucky as much as Lucky needs him; even before that, Pozzo claims that he learned all he knows from his slave.

Vladimir and Estragon enjoy watching and playing Pozzo and Lucky. In this way the latter pseudocouple's passage on the stage functions as a play within the play, mirroring in condensed—and even more grotesque—form the absurd situation of Vladimir and Estragon. This metatheatrical dimension emerges at other moments in *Waiting for Godot*. For example, Pozzo asks whether the place where they find themselves is called "the Board"—theatrical jargon for the stage (WFG 55); our heroes echo what impatient spectators must think when they say, "Nothing happens, nobody comes, nobody goes, it's awful" and "This is becoming really insignificant" (WFG 27, 44); the compliment is returned when Vladimir, pointing toward the audience, tells Estragon to run in that direction because there's "not a soul in sight" (WFG 47). When Vladimir leaves the stage to go to the men's room, it is clear they know they are not in the country, but in a theater. Estragon tells Vladimir the toilet is at the "end of the corridor, on the left," and Vladimir asks him to "keep my seat" (WFG 23). Indeed, the first words of *Waiting for Godot,* Estragon's famous line, "Nothing to be done," regarding his hopelessly uncomfortable shoes, summarizes the action—or lack thereof—of the entire play.

Endgame

Beckett's next drama, *Fin de partie (Endgame),* first performed in 1957, is even more metatheatrical than *Waiting for Godot.* Indeed, the word *game* in its title belongs to the same semantic field as "play." As the performance begins, we see a bare interior, with two windows, high up, covered by curtains. A man with a laborious walk—we later learn his name is Clov— comes onstage, pulls a stepladder up to each window, and opens the curtains, thus representing within the play the start of the performance. He also removes cloths from the other furnishings, as a stagehand takes the dust covers off the set before the play begins. The first items revealed are two garbage cans at the front left. Clov takes the lid off one of them, peers inside, smiles, closes the lid, and then repeats these actions with the other can. His movements are extremely methodical, and an actor with a good sense of timing can make them funny; this is another example of Beckett's comic use of the human reduced to the mechanical. Finally Clov removes the cloth from the centerpiece of the scene and we see a man, apparently asleep, in a straight- back chair on castor wheels, his face hidden—yet more covering!—by a blood-stained handkerchief. Later we learn he is Hamm, Clov's blind and paralyzed master. He cannot stand, and Clov cannot sit. They comple- ment each other's infirmities, as befits a pseudocouple.

So far, no words have been uttered. This is em- blematic of the silence that constantly encroaches upon the play. In *Waiting for Godot* the stage direction "Pause" occurred often, but it is even more frequent here, where the breakdown of language is pushed even further. This

is apparent when Clov, after his many initial movements, at last speaks the opening line: "Finished, it's
finished, nearly finished, it must be nearly finished."
On a purely sonorous level the repetition of words tends
to wear away sense; on a syntactic level the sentence
works through many fragments ("Finished, it's finished,
nearly finished") until it reaches its no more than tentative message: "it must be nearly finished." It is on
the semantic level that these words are most problematic:
how are we to understand that a play lasting over an
hour should start by announcing that it is almost over?

Later on, Hamm will echo Clov's opening words:
"The end is in the beginning an yet you go on" (E 69).
Paradoxical as this idea is, it is not unfamiliar. When
a child is born, its fate is sealed; it will someday die
and return to the inanimate state from which it emerged.
Moreover, if the nineteenth-century evolutionist Haeckel
(mentioned by name in *How It Is* [H 42]) said, "Ontogeny recapitulates phylogeny," with respect to *Endgame*
we have to say that phylogeny recapitulates ontogeny.
Not only does the individual's development mirror that
of the species, but the life of the species follows that of
the individual: if the individual dies, so can the species. This seems to be what has happened in *Endgame,*
which shows us a day in the lives of the last survivors
of a giant catastrophe, presumably a nuclear war, in
which all forms of life have been wiped out: "There's
no more nature," says Clov (E 11). Hamm says, "The
whole place stinks of corpses," and Clov replies, "The
whole universe" (E 46).

The end of humankind is figured onstage by the
two garbage cans, for each contains a person who has
been disposed of. From the cans emerge the heads and

torsos of Negg and Nell, Hamm's father and mother. They lost their legs at Sedan, in the Ardennes between France and Belgium, as a result of an accident on their tandem, a bicycle built for two. Theodor Adorno, the social theoretician of the Frankfurt school, argues in an article on *Endgame* that the reference to the Ardennes mountains is significant, for they were the site of one of the first modern mass destructions, the battlegrounds of World War I.[4] No less symbolic is the fate befalling the bicycle. For Beckett's Molloy this vehicle had been a marvel, extending the human body, but for Nagg and Nell it has become an instrument of destruction. Hamm, who harbors no small amount of hostility toward his "accursed progenitor" (E 9), has a warm spot in his heart for bicycles, wishing he had a "proper wheel-chair. With big wheels. Bicycle wheels!" (E 25). But as befits a world at end, there are no more bicycle wheels; we also learn, at various points, that there are no more tides, bowls of porridge, sugarplums, coffins, navigators, rugs, Turkish delight (a kind of candy), or plaid blankets to cover Hamm's useless legs.

Life in this postholocaust world is quite painful. Hamm repeatedly asks Clov for a pain-killer, and Clov always answers that the time for it has not yet come. until the end when he informs him, "There's no more pain-killer" (E 71). These words apply to the audience as well: we share the characters' pain as spectators of the terribly laborious dialogue and action. We cannot escape from the fact that existence is painful, and that our world is bent on destruction.

By having the audience not simply observe but undergo a carefully orchestrated ritual of cruelty, Beckett follows the precepts of Antonin Artaud, who urged that modern theater leave realism behind and look toward classical Greek theater and its origins in ritual. Sacrifice is the most dramatic of rituals, and it is an important part of *Endgame,* where all of humankind is offered up in empty holocaust to a God of whom Hamm says, "The bastard! he doesn't exist" (E 55).

The concept of an imperfect world sacrificed to a nonexistent creator is figured in a desperate joke told by Nagg, in a failed attempt to make Nell laugh. Like much in Beckett, this joke is tremendously repetitious; Nagg is said to have told it to her endless times, and in his recounting of it he uses repetition to rhetorical purposes. The joke is even a repetition for Beckett, who has already used it in an essay on painting (D 118). The story is about a tailor who works on a pair of pants for several months. At the end the customer is irate: "In six days, do you hear me, six days, God made the world. yes Sir, no less Sir, the WORLD! And you are not bloody well capable of making me a pair of trousers in three months!" (E 22). The tailor responds, scandalized: "But my dear Sir, my dear Sir, look—at the world—and look— at my TROUSERS!"

Adorno tells us that this is a Jewish joke, a fact not irrelevant in a play that deals with the aftermath of a holocaust.[5] We never learn the exact nature of the catastrophe that brought humankind to its end, and Adorno explains this reticence as reflecting the fact that the unspeakable tends only to be referred to indirectly, "the way people in Germany speak of the murder of the Jews."[6] He also notes a more practical consideration: if the destruction were addressed directly, it would introduce an element of lurid science-fiction interest.

Whatever the nature of the catastrophe, Hamm seems to have played an important role in it. For example, asked by Hamm whether a certain doctor has perished, Clov replies "naturally" (E 25), surprised that Hamm should wonder, as though no one knew better than he about the death of all. Likewise, when Clov discovers a flea on himself, Hamm orders him to exterminate it immediately, lest "humanity [. . .] start from there all over again" (E 33). In exaggerated frenzy Clov obeys, repeatedly pouring insecticide powder into his own pants. (We are reminded that for the Nazis, Jews were vermin.)

Such overreaction on Clov's part (if we can speak of overreaction in such an extreme universe) has led commentators to see in Clov's name a form of the word *clown,* just as Hamm's name can be seen as a reference to his ham acting, his love of flourish. The question in his opening lines—"Can there be misery—loftier than mine?"—is typical in this respect. Another critical tradition interprets the names with respect to the relationship between the characters. Hamm would be the *hamm*er, merciless against all humanity, who bears down on several nails: his slave Clov (*clou* in French means nail), his father Nagg (*Nagel* is German for nail), and his mother Nell (whose name sounds like nail). An old woman to whom Hamm once refused aid is named Mother *Pegg*. Nailing is of course part of another sacrifice central to humankind: the Crucifixion. Thus some commentators have likened Clov's opening of *Endgame* ("Finished, it's finished") to Jesus' words on the cross: "It is finished" (John 19:30).

Clov does not simply say "It's finished," but goes

on to say, "nearly finished," and this "nearly" provides the space in which the play can occur. These characters await the imminent end no less surely than Vladimir and Estragon await Godot, but there is a difference. There is an element of suspense in the first play. Even though Godot never comes, it is possible to imagine that he could come; indeed, many lives are spent waiting for a deliverance that never occurs. Some critics have suggested that *Endgame* provides a similar sense of drama, in that we are waiting to find out whether Clov will actually leave Hamm, as he claims he will do many times. However, given the universal barrenness, it is clear that this is an empty threat, another instance of the wearing-away of language throughout this play.

At one point it seems life could exist on the outside. Clov looks through the window and believes he sights a boy. He plans to go off to kill the "potential procreator" as he did the flea, but Hamm urges the boy be paid no heed: "If he exists he'll die there or he'll come here. And if he doesn't ..." (E 78). Unlike the messenger at the end of *Godot,* the boy here not only offers no hope, but constitutes a danger or a mirage. The characters can envisage no positive change. There is basically no suspense in *Endgame;* the sole thing they could possibly be awaiting will definitely come: it is death.

But death is something that, in a sense, never comes. Wait for it as we like, when it arrives we have died and cannot know it has arrived. This is the paradox Beckett's Malone is painfully aware of, as are the characters of *Endgame.* They speak of it in terms of the logical impossibility of reaching an endpoint, formulated in antiquity by Zeno. This ancient Greek imagined that a man nearing a certain point first goes half the distance there. Then he goes half the remaining distance, and he is three-quarters of the way there. He goes half the remaining distance, and he is seven-eighths there. It is clear that reasoned this way, the end can never be reached.

Clov speaks of this problem in the second sentence he utters: "Grain upon grain, one by one, and one day, suddenly, there's a heap, a little heap, the impossible heap." That is to say, at what point does a grain-by-grain accumulation of sand become a heap? Like much else in *Endgame* this is repeated. Hamm says, toward the close of the play: "Moment upon moment, pattering down, like the millet grains of . . . that old Greek, and all life long you wait for that to mount up to a life" (E 70—the "old Greek" refers to Zeno). It is perhaps Hamm's knowledge of this paradox that leads him to doubt anything can end:

Hamm:	No more pain-killer!
Clov:	No more pain-killer. You'll never get any more pain-killer.
	(*Pause*)
Hamm:	But the little round box. It was full!
Clov:	Yes. But now it's empty. (E 71)

It seems impossible for anything to finish in *Endgame,* for if all human life ceased, there would be nothingness, not an "end." In order that there be an end, a subjectivity is required to notice the ending; ends do not exist in themselves. That is why a world, even an imagined one, without God, without humans, is impossible. That is why, in the only science-fiction moment of this play, Hamm imagines what would happen "if a rational being came back to earth, wouldn't he be liable to get ideas into his head if he observed us long enough" (E 33). The look of the other, as Sartre would say, is necessary to make us exist. That is what is funny about Clov's turning his telescope on the audience and saying "I see ... a multitude ... in transports ... of joy" (E 29). This comment—ironic in terms of the play's pretense that these four characters are the last survivors on earth—not only reminds us we are watching a play; it makes it clear that we need imagine the impossible world in which there could be no one watching.

Humans cannot really end, they can only play at ending. This is one resonance of the title *Endgame.* Actually "endgame" is a term taken from chess, where it designates the final stage of a game, when few pieces are left on the board. The chess metaphor has led to the comparison of Hamm to a king and of Clov, Nagg, and Nell to his pawns. Hamm's blindness and hubris have made him seem like King Lear, and other Shakespearean echoes—his saying "My kingdom for a nightman" and "Our revels now are ended" (E 23, 56)—have caused critics to see in him versions of King Richard III (5.4.7: "My kingdom for a horse"), and Prospero (in *The Tempest,* 4.1.148: "Our revels now are ended").[7] Hamm asks if the words "Mene, mene" appear before him (E 12), thereby likening himself to the biblical king Belshazzar, who saw the proverbial writing on the wall. The prophet Daniel interpreted these enigmatic words as "God hath numbered thy kingdom, and finished it" (Daniel 5:26).

Hamm's kingship would explain the major role that seems to have been his in the universal holocaust. The reduction of his domain to the court held in his shelter is underscored when he instructs Hamm to take him "for a little turn. [. . .] Right round the world!" (E 25). Since the inhabitable world consists of no more than one room, the obedient Clove grazes its walls with Hamm's wheelchair, and brings him back to his original position. Hamm wants to make sure he is in the center of his universe, like the sun in its. This treats us to one of the play's mechanically repetitive moments:

Hamm: I feel a little too far to the left.
           (Clov moves chair slightly.)
           Now I feel a little too far to the right.
           (Clov moves chair slightly.)
           I feel a little too far forward.
           (Clov moves chair slightly.)
           Now I feel a little too far back.
           (Clov moves chair slightly.) (E 27).

However, there are passages in the play that make us doubt whether Hamm was so important in the world before the catastrophe. Like Godot, who at certain moments appears to be a divine agency or even God himself and at others a powerful but earthly authority, so Hamm seems at times to be the Antichrist who caused Armageddon and at others a squire like Pozzo, blind like Pozzo; his sin may have not been to exterminate billions but simply the banal one of disregarding suffering. For example, accused by Clov of causing a death by refusing to give oil to a neighbor, Hamm excoriates himself with Pozzo-like flourish: "All those I might have helped. *(Pause.)* Helped! *(Pause.)* Saved. *(Pause.)* Saved!" (E 68).

Like Vladimir, Hamm is the crueler member of the pseudocouple:

Hamm:	I'll give you nothing more to eat.
Clov:	Then we'll die.
Hamm:	I'll give you just enough to keep you from dying. You'll be hungry all the time.
Clov:	Then we won't die. (E 5–6)

This kind of exchange, where Clov gives the same answer both affirmatively and negatively, occurs when he formulates his vague plan to leave:

Clov:	So you all want me to leave you.
Hamm:	Naturally.
Clov:	Then I'll leave you.
Hamm:	You can't leave us.
Clov:	Then I won't leave you. (E 37)

The same affirmative/negative switch occurs when Hamm tells Clov to look to see if Nagg and Nell are dead. Peering into Nell's ashcan, Clov says, "Looks like it," and opening up Nagg's, he says, "Doesn't look like it" (E 62). This rapid shift between opposites, uttered in the same tone as though there were no difference between leaving and staying, living and dying, is another example of the terrible disintegration of existence and language. The same occurs when Clov reduces fatherhood and home to the empty pronouns *this* and *that:*

Hamm:	I was a father to you.
Clov:	Yes.
	(He looks at Hamm fixedly.)
	You were that to me.
Hamm:	My house a home for you.
Clov:	Yes.
	(He looks about him.)
	This was that for me. (E 38)

In *Waiting for Godot,* Beckett had already fragmented language terribly in Vladimir's and Estragon's exchange of short responses, but in *Endgame* the characters address each other in an even choppier manner. Didi and Gogo may be allowed to use language a bit more thoughtfully, less automatically, because they have a purpose—they are waiting for Godot—whereas Hamm and Clov are allowed no such illusions; they know there is no reason for them to go on. "What is there to keep me here?" asks Clov. Hamm responds, "The dialogue" (E 58). This is, of course, yet another of the play's references to itself, but it is not simply that. We have all had the sensation of being in conversations that continue on their own steam, because we have had them

140

before. Thus one of the most famous exchanges between Hamm and Clov: "What's happening?" "Something is taking its course" (E 32). Likewise: "Why this farce, day after day?" asks Clov, and Hamm answers, "Routine" (E 32). So meager are the conversations that Hamm is reduced to describing his own actions each time he brings a new prop onto the set: "I'm back again, with the biscuit"; "I'm back again, with the glass"; "I'm back again, with the steps"; "I'm back again, with the insecticide" (E 10, 28, 34). If Vladimir had to urge Estragon to do his part to keep conversation flowing ("Come on, Gogo, return the ball, can't you, once in a way?" [WFG 91]), Hamm goes on step further and actually tells Clov what to ask him. Then, to prolong the verbal exchange, he pretends he does not know what Clov is referring to:

Hamm:	I've got on with my story.
	(Pause.)
	I've got on with it well.
	(Pause. Irritably.)
	Ask me where I've got to.
Clov:	Oh, by the way, your story?
Hamm (surprised): What story?
Clov:	The one you've been telling yourself all your days.
Hamm:	Ah you mean my chronicle?
Clov:	That's the one. *(Pause.)*
Hamm (angrily): Keep going, can't you, keep going!
Clov:	You've got on with it, I hope. (E 58–59)

In this passage Hamm acts like an irascible stage director, coaxing a recalcitrant and uninspired actor. The story itself, like much else in this play, refers to the situation at hand. Hamm tells of a man who came begging for food and whose son he takes into his service. We suspect immediately that this is the story behind his association with Clov.

Like Vladimir's philosophical disquisitions in *Godot*—and their parody in Lucky's "think"—Hamm's tale is one of the counterpoints to the often staccato dialogue. But there is a difference between the use of the same technique in both plays: whereas Vladimir's and Lucky's monologues present thought, ill conceived or automatic as it may be, Hamm wishes to provide entertainment, as did his father with the tailor joke. Like Pozzo spraying his throat before speaking in *Godot,* Hamm marks a distinction between his conversational speech and his declamatory tone:

The man came crawling towards me, on his belly. Pale, wonderfully pale and thin, he seemed on the point of—

(Pause. Normal tone.)

No, I've done that bit.

(Pause. Narrative tone.)

I calmly filled my pipe—the meerschaum, lit it with ... let us say a vesta, drew a few puffs. Aah!

(Pause.)

Well, what is it *you* want? (E 50–51)

Like the joke told by Nagg, Hamm recounts the story as a conversation, both of whose parts he enacts; the dialogic form makes it into a playlet within the play. Moreover, we are presented not only with the exchanges between Hamm and Clov's father but also those between Hamm the character and Hamm the narrator, between Hamm the (ham) actor and Hamm the director:

> It was a glorious bright day, I remember, fifty by the heliometer, but already the sun was sinking down into the ... down among the dead.
>
> *(Normal tone.)*
>
> Nicely put, that.
>
> *(Narrative tone.)*
>
> Come on now, come on, present your petition and let me resume my labors.
>
> *(Pause. Normal tone.)*
>
> There's English for you. (E 51)

The expression Hamm admires himself for using—"Come on now, come on, present your petition and let me resume my labors"—is reminiscent of the Bible (Isaiah 1:18: "Come now, let us reason together") and Shakespeare (*Hamlet* 1.2.58–59: "He hath, my lord, wrung from me my slow leave/ By laborsome petition"). Variations on Hamm's description of the weather—"It was a glorious bright day, I remember, fifty by the heliometer"—which he finds to be "nicely put," form a refrain throughout his story:

143

It was an extra-ordinarily bitter day, I remember, zero by the thermometer (E 51).

It was a howling wild day, I remember, a hundred by the anenometer (E 52).

It was an exceedingly dry day, I remember, zero by the hygrometer (E 53).

What could be the meaning of this refrain? That through the use of measuring instruments man has alienated himself even from weather? Or does the effect of these lines reside primarily in their careful rhythm, in accordance with Beckett's beliefs that the shape of an idea is more important than its sense and that his work is a matter of fundamental sounds? The author of the present work can assure the reader that he was haunted by this refrain for years, after forgetting its source, and that he rediscovered it with great glee when he returned to *Endgame* as a serious student of Beckett.

Hamm's story of the boy left with him is taken up in what he calls his "last soliloquy" (E 78), performed as Clov watches, dressed for the trip he will likely not take. As Hamm begins, he makes the only explicit reference to the chess metaphor in the title—"old endgame lost of old, play and lose and have done with losing" (E 82)—and the presages the curtain fall with a line loosely adapted from the nineteenth-century French poet Charles Baudelaire: "You cried for night; it falls: now cry in darkness" (E 83; the original poem, *Recueillement,* reads: "Tu réclamais le Soir; il descend; le voici" [v. 2]).

Hamm then says that "time was never and time is over, reckoning closed and story ended" (E 83). That

time should be both over and never have been is contradictory but not illogical: if time has ended, we are
in a timeless dimension; therefore it is impossible for
time to have existed before, for there could be no "before." What exists does so in eternal simultaneity, as
in a myth so much a part of our heritage that all its
elements seem present to us. Oedipus' murder of his
father takes place before his marriage to his mother,
the ten plagues occur prior to the giving of the Ten
Commandments, yet for us all these events have never
stopped. Thus Pascal conceived of the Crucifixion as
eternal: "Jesus will be in agony even to the end of the
world."[8]

The same is true of the myths created by Beckett.
Even if we can imagine Godot coming, Didi and Gogo
will always be waiting for him; Hamm and Clov will
always be "nearly finished," although in a world where
there are no more coffins, Turkish delight, or porridge,
it only stands to reason that there should someday be
no more Hamm and Clov. Hence, though Hamm deems
the "reckoning closed and story ended," he returns to
his final tale. He recounts how he ridiculed Clov's father,
who hesitated to leave his son, by asking whether the
boy was to be "there to solace your last million last
moments" (E 83). "Last million last moments" suggests
that one has almost died a million times, and one will
continue to do so. Indeed, is not life an endless series
of moments all of which could have been the last? We
live in an eternal imminence of the end, which keeps
the end forever at bay.

Thus when the play "ends," it actually returns to
its beginning. The last lines of Hamm's soliloquy and
of the play are "Old stancher! *(Pause.)* You ... remain"

(E 84). He pronounces these words as he places a blood-stained handkerchief on his face; at the start of the play he had removed the handkerchief from his face, saying, "Old stancher!" (E 2). Critic Ruby Cohn sees in this cloth an avatar of the one Veronica used to wipe Jesus' face and which retained his image.[9] Jean-Jacques Mayoux[10] finds another reference to the Crucifixion in the final soliloquy when Hamm, imitating the boy, calls out "Father! *(Pause. Louder.)* Father!" (E 84): on the cross Jesus cried out, "My God, my God, why hast thou forsaken me?" (Matthew 27:46; Mark 15:34). These words attest to Jesus' humanity; momentarily even he doubts God. Like the characters in *Endgame,* he might have said to himself: "The bastard! He doesn't exist!"

All That Fall

It is strange to consider that Beckett's radio play *All That Fall* (1957), the first work he originally wrote in English since the novel *Watt* in 1944, was composed at approximately the same time as *Endgame. Endgame* presents an absurd world reduced to its last survivors, whereas *All That Fall* is a basically realistic play, taking place in Ireland in the 1930s. It follows Mrs. Maddy Rooney, an old middle-class woman, as she wends her way slowly through a village, going to meet her blind husband's train. She comes successively upon several men, as old and decrepit as herself, with whom she vaguely flirts; two laborers who help her along; and a prude named Miss Fitt. The train comes in late, her husband Dan finally arrives, and they begin their journey homeward. Their conversation takes many odd turns, of which the strangest is no doubt this remark by Mr. Rooney: "Did you ever wish to kill a child? *(Pause.)* Nip some young doom in the bud" (CSP 31). Just before the end of the play a young man who had guided Mr. Rooney on the train runs up with an object Mr. Rooney had left behind in the men's room: it seems to be a small ball, such as children play with. Thereupon Mrs. Rooney asks why the train came in late; the reason, of which Mr. Rooney claims total ignorance, is that a child had been run over. The play abruptly ends, and we are left with the suspicion that Mr. Rooney may have taken the ball from a child he pushed onto the tracks,.

Reading or hearing the play a second time, we see how carefully Beckett prepares us for this ending. Childlessness and the death of children are recurrent themes. For example, a mother is overheard warning a child to stay far from the railroad tracks; Mrs. Rooney mentioned a daughter who died young, saying that she would now be in her forties, "getting ready for the change" of life, when she could no longer have children (CSP 16); the first man Mrs. Rooney meets on the way to the station, Mr. Tyler, has a daughter who is sterile because of a hysterectomy: "They removed everything, you know, the whole ... er ... bag of tricks. Now I am grandchildless" (CSP 14). Mr. Tyler even regrets his own birth, "cursing, under [his] breath, [...] the wet Saturday of [his] conception" (CSP 15). Later on, Mrs. Rooney tells the story of a famed medical specialist she heard speak on the case of a young girl who died because "she had never really been born" (CSP 36). Even animal infertility occupies Mrs. Rooney's mind. She wonders whether "hinnies"—animals similar to mules— "can procreate": "aren't they barren, or sterile, or whatever it is?" (CSP 37); and she mourns the loss of the potential offspring of a chicken she sees run over.

Childlessness means lack of posthumous existence, but Mrs. Rooney throws into question even her present one. She says to one of the men she comes upon: "Don't mind me. Don't take any notice of me. I do not exist. The fact is well known" (CSP 19). To another she says, "I was so plunged in sorrow that I wouldn't have heard a steam roller go over me" (CSP 21). Mrs. Rooney does not exist for others as well. The prudish Miss Fitt fails to greet her, claiming to be so absorbed in her pious thoughts that she sees only an indistinct shape. Mrs. Rooney, perhaps only half-ironically, reflects upon herself in Miss Fitt's eyes: "Maddy Rooney, née Dunne, the big pale blur" (CSP 23). The names, as always in Beckett, are suggestive. "Maddy" indicates she might be a little off mentally: she calls herself "hysterical" (CSP 14), a word that suggests reproductive problems in that it derives from the same Greek root as *uterus*. Her name reminds us that she had been a mother (*Ma*ddy), and Mr. Rooney's, that he had been a father (*Da*n). Yet they are failed parents, their daughter having died; whence, perhaps, their deformed names, similar to those Molloy gave to his parents, Da and Mag (TN 17).

It is significant that Maddy is "née Dunne," that is, born Dunne, born done for—like the patient whom the great specialist diagnosed as never having been properly born. Such a diagnosis is less rare than might appear, since it applies to all of us: we are never properly born into life, for life is a road to death. The name Rooney underscores such congenital *ruin*ation; in the very first line of the play the syllable *ruin* is uttered, as Maddy evokes a woman whose fate is no happier

148

than her own: "Poor woman. All alone in that ruinous old house."

Not only are individual deaths evoked; so is mass catastrophe. Mrs. Rooney remarks how "touching" it must have been that passengers on the doomed ships *Lusitania* and *Titanic* sang hymns (CSP 24). The uselessness of such appeals to God motivates the play's title, for the words come from a psalm quoted by Maddy as the subject of a sermon by her preacher: "The Lord upholdeth all that fall and raiseth up all those that be bowed down" (CSP 38; see Psalm 145:14). The title mentions the falling and leaves out the raising up, as befits these souls moving toward childless deaths.

The degradation of the characters is accompanied by the wearing-away of language. Mr. Rooney wonders about his wife's and his own ungainly grammar:

Mrs. Rooney:	There is nothing to be done for those people!
Mr. Rooney:	For which is there? *(Pause.)* That does not sound right somehow. (CSP 36)
Mrs. Rooney:	It's like the sparrows, than many of which we are of more value [. . .].
Mr. Rooney:	Than many of which! . . . You exaggerate, Maddy. (CSP 37)

Mrs. Rooney had already remarked that her speech is unusual, asking her helper Christy:

Do you find anything . . . bizarre about my way of speaking? *(Pause.)* I do not mean the voice. *(Pause.)*

149

No, I mean the words. *(Pause. More to herself.)* I use none but the simplest words, I hope, and yet I sometimes find my way of speaking very ... bizarre (CSP 13).

This description corresponds not only to Maddy's speech but also to Beckett's style throughout his oeuvre, starting with the switch to French. The simplest words are used, but they are combined in the strangest ways. *All That Fall* contains the dialogue analyzed above in chapter 1, where the characters, feeling the strangeness of their own English words, have the impression of speaking a dead language.

The themes of *All That Fall*—sterility of the old and the death of the young, the wearing-away of language—show how close this play is to *Endgame,* despite the difference in setting: the seeds of destruction exist within everyday life. There is, however, a more apparent similarity between the two plays: in each the male protagonist, the one responsible for the tragedy (the sacrifice of a child or of an entire universe), is blind.

Hamm's and Dan's lack of vision relates them to the great tragic hero Oedipus. Sophocles' *Oedipus the King* portrays the aftermath of the plague at Thebes, and *Endgame* recounts what follows even more general destruction. Likewise, the ancient myth tells the story of Oedipus as a child, who was to be killed to avoid catastrophe (the fulfillment of the prophecy that he would kill his father and marry his mother); *All That Fall* reveals the murder of a child "in order to nip some young doom in the bud," in accordance with the classical wisdom evoked by Nietzsche at the beginning of *The Birth of Tragedy:* "What is best of all is ... not to be born. . . . But the second best for you is—to die soon."[11]

In a radio play blindness corresponds to our situation as listeners, who cannot see what is going on; in this way we resemble not only the blind Mr. Rooney but also Mr. Slocum, a stalled motorist whom Mrs. Rooney observes "gazing straight [. . .] through the windscreen, into the void" (csp 18).

The noise of the failing automobile, reflecting the sounds of the decrepit characters moving along, is one of the sources of vaudevillesque humor in *All That Fall*. As critic Linda Ben-Zvi has noted, in this radio play Beckett had to use sound to achieve the comical effects attained with stage numbers in *Waiting for Godot*.[12] Another critic, Robert Wilcher, has pointed to a more unusual use of sound in *All That Fall*.[13] Mrs. Rooney evokes natural phenomena *before* we hear the noises associated with them:

> The wind—*(Brief wind.)*—scarcely stirs the leaves and the birds—*(Brief chirp.)*—are tired singing. The cows—*(Brief moo.)*—and sheep—*(Brief baa.)*—ruminate in silence. The dogs—*(Brief bark.)*—are hushed and the hens—*(Brief cackle.)*—sprawl torpid in the dust. We are alone. There is no one to ask (csp 32).

Contrary to the myth that language originated when humans imitated the sounds of nature, here language appears as primary, calling forth natural sounds. As Beckett reminded us in his essay on Dante and Joyce, Genesis does not say that God gave language to man; rather, man invented language: "'the animals were given names by Adam,' the man who 'first said goo to a goose'" (d 31). We project our own sounds onto the

151

world, even onto beasts, as is proven by the fact that in the several languages different words denote the cries of the same animals. God is not the guarantor of language; man himself is. Hence Mrs. Rooney's last words in her speech above: "We are alone. There is no one to ask." That the absence of God is evoked in a radio play is significant. The divine voice that the prophets heard crashing from the heavens has been transformed in our time into the human voice traveling through the airwaves. We fall, and have not the God who will raise us up.

Beckett wrote another radio play in English shortly after *All That Fall.* This was *Embers,* first broadcast by the BBC in 1959. *Embers* shares many of the themes and techniques of the earlier play. For example, the protagonist, Henry, calls out the noises he wants to hear—hooves, water dripping—and they are miraculously produced, like Mrs. Rooney's animal cries. And if Mr. Rooney's blindness corresponds to the situation of the radio listener, so the voices Henry hears in his head are as disembodied as those the audience is presented with. An ironic touch is added by the titled *Embers,* given to a work whose dominant sound is the crash of the sea. But this name is by no means as surprising as that of the next Beckett play we shall consider.

Krapp's Last Tape

Krapp's Last Tape (1958) is the first work Beckett wrote in English for the theater rather than the airwaves, yet in it as well voice comes to the fore. Its action is simple: the old down-and-outer Krapp listens in shabby surroundings to a tape he recorded some thirty years before, and then records a new one. A few other things occur, mostly in the beginning: Krapp goes through his pockets, takes out an envelope, puts it back, takes out his keys, opens his desk drawers, rummages through them, finds bananas, and eats them. Krapp is clownlike in his exaggerated movements, his ragged clothes, his large shoes. The banana eating includes the inevitable vaudeville bit of his slipping on a peel. He also runs backstage twice, to drink a bottle of beer; the sound of the uncorking invariably elicits laughter.

Since Krapp possesses a great many tapes, he has catalogued them in a ledger. From it he reads forth the summary of the recording we shall hear this evening. It treats of his mother's death, an affair with a "dark nurse," a "slight improvement in [his] bowel condition," a "memorable equinox," and his "farewell to [. . .] love" (CSP 57). Krapp begins to play the tape, and on it we hear a more youthful version of his voice. It is his thirty-ninth birthday, the midpoint of his life, "the crest of the wave—or thereabouts" (CSP 57). The younger Krapp already does many of the things the old one will do: he eats bananas, jots down notes on the back of envelopes, and listens to tapes of himself from earlier times: "Just been listening to an old year [. . .]. Hard to believe I was ever that young whelp" (CSP 58). This is a perfectly recursive structure, what the French call a *mise en abyme:* Krapp listens to himself having listened to himself.

The thirty-nine-year-old begins recounting an amorous adventure, the one that must have led to his "farewell to love." The older Krapp, impatient, stops, advances, and restarts the tape, listens for a while, then takes it off in mid-stream. He puts on a blank tape and begins recording. His first words are a variation on the self-deprecating comments the younger Krapp had already used to refer to an even earlier self: "Just been listening to that stupid bastard I took myself for thirty years ago, hard to believe I was ever as bad as that" (CSP 62). The recursive structure is pushed even further: not only does Krapp listen to himself having listened to himself; he records himself having listened to himself recording himself having listened to himself.

Yet there are differences between the Krapps. The thirty-nine-year-old speaks vaguely of a great work: "Shadows of the opus ... magnum" (CSP 58), whereas the old man has written the masterpiece, to little avail: the book sold fewer than twenty copies. Also, the old Krapp has accepted sexual life in its least romantic form: "Fanny came in a couple of times. Bony old ghost of a whore" (CSP 62), whereas the thirty-nine-year-old (whose tape old Krapp replaces on the machine) evokes in ever greater detail the moment of amorous bliss he experienced with a woman in a boat: "We lay there without moving. But under us all moved, and moved us, gently, up and down, and from side to side" (CSP 63). Yet as the play ends, the recorder recounts the younger man's renunciation of love for an apparently higher good: "Perhaps my best years are gone. When there was a chance of happiness. But I wouldn't want them back. Not with the fire in me now. No, I wouldn't want them back" (CSP 63).

The "fire" seems to be that of artistic inspiration, worth more to the thirty-nine-year-old Krapp than the flames of love. The question remains whether he did well to be guided by the muses rather than by Eros;

after all, he failed as an artist. Yet given the fate of love in other works by Beckett, we can be sure that Krapp's would have been a fiasco as well. He may have done better to fail as an artist, if we consider a statement Beckett made when he was about the same age as the Krapp on tape: "To be an artist is to fail, as no other dare fail"; the artist must make of failure "an expressive act, even if only of itself" (D 145).

If the best one can do is fail felicitously as an artist, it might be better never to have been born at all, as Beckett suggests in *All That Fall*. Thus Krapp, speaking of his birthday, says he "celebrated the awful occasion" (CSP 57), and he is attracted to an image of death in birth, a nursemaid pushing "a big black hooded perambulator, most funereal thing" (CSP 59). One might as well begin mourning while the child is still in the carriage. As our hero's name suggests, life is crap.

Excrement, as we saw in our reading of *How It Is,* functions as part-object. The child, becoming toilet trained, learns to relate to excrement as a part of himself that has become other than himself. The name Krapp is appropriate not only because its bearer is plagued by constipation ("unattainable laxation" [CSP 58]), but also because he invests other part-objects, separated from their original context. To start with the most obvious: the bananas Krapp eats represent disembodied penises. He always peels the bananas entirely before eating them, separating the fruit into two objects; this operation is evoked, figuratively, by the younger Krapp who speaks of "separating the grain from the husks," sorting out his life before a fire (CSP 57). Separation is clear in Krapp's habit of jotting down notes on the backs of envelopes, presumably emptied of their contents. One can even see this act, whereby Krapp writes letters to himself, as a form of retention, relating to his constipation.

Krapp's letters in another sense—his books—function as part-objects: rather than forming part of a literary corpus, they are dispersed: "Seventeen copies sold, of which eleven at trade price to free circulating libraries beyond the seas" (CSP 62). Likewise, the exaggerated size of his feet separate them from the rest of his body, and the nursemaid he finds attractive is referred to in parts: "The face she had! The eyes!" (CSP 60).

Another part-object is Krapp's voice, captivating him in its disembodied form, as recording. The recipient of the voice—the spool of tape—assumes as well a life of its own: Krapp calls the tape a "little rascal" or a "little scoundrel" when he cannot find it (CSP 56). In the French translation, where the word for spool—*bobine*—is of feminine gender, Beckett has Krapp call it a "coquine," a hussy. The sexual overtones are especially important in French, where the title, *La Dernière Bande,* means not only "The Last Tape" but "The Last Hard-On." Indeed, the play deals with Krapp's last great love; moreover, the separation of Krapp's erection from himself in the French title (not *"Krapp's* Last Hard-On" but *"The* Last Hard-on") is suggestive of the role of part-objects in the play.

Not only Krapp's voice but the words he uses function as part-objects, separated from their context and meaning. We see this in the first lines of the play, as Krapp reads from the entry in his ledger of tapes: "Box . . . thrree *[sic]* . . . spool . . . five *(He raises his head and stares front. With relish.)* Spool! *(Pause.)* Spooool! *(Happy smile)*" (csp 56). A few lines later he lovingly pronounces the word "spool" again; and when he starts taping himself, he says that he "revelled again in the word spool. *(With relish.)* Spooool! Happiest moment of the past half million" (csp 62).

Krapp is able to enjoy the written as well as the spoken word. Hearing his younger self's reactions to his mother's death "after her long viduity" (csp 59), the old Krapp replays that portion of the tape, mouthing the syllables of the rare word. Thereupon he stops the tape, goes backstage, and brings out an enormous dictionary from which he reads this definition of "viduity":

> State—or condition—of being—or remaining—a widow—or widower. *(Looks up. Puzzled.)* Being—or remaining? ... *(Pause. He peers again at dictionary. Reading.)* "Deep weeds of viduity." ... Also of an animal, especially a bird.... The vidua or weaverbird.... Black plumage of male.... *(He looks up. With relish.)* The vidua-bird! (csp 59).

The word *viduity* is enjoyed, separated from its context, in a dictionary; Krapp had used it to refer to his mother, separated from her husband by his death; now her death has taken her from Krapp.

The part-objects—words, voice, bananas, keys, empty envelopes, the grain separated from the husks, the isolated parts of Krapp's and his beloved's bodies, the tapes as depositories of disembodied voices—all are representatives of the great Separator, Death itself. Thus Krapp evokes the separation of himself from his own body, disseminated as dust: "The grain, now what I wonder do I mean by that, I mean ... *(hesitates)* ... I suppose I mean those things worth having when all the dust has—

when all *my* dust has settled" (CSP 57). Beckett, in his own production of *Krapp's Last Tape,* rendered death palpable by having Krapp gaze, with fear, into the dark. "Death is waiting behind him and, says Beckett, unconsciously he is seeking it: 'He's through with his work, with love and with religion'".[14] The same is *not* true of Beckett's protagonist in *Happy Days* (1961), who despite being buried alive manages to remain optimistic.

Happy Days

Krapp's Last Tape presents a difficult task to the actor. He must perform what is essentially a monologue while manipulating a tape recorder, even if the taped voice does not actually emanate from the recorder on the set but is rather controlled by offstage personnel. *Happy Days,* which debuted in 1961, provides a possibly greater challenge to its main performer.

The play opens on a barren outdoor setting, brightly lit, in which we sight a woman around forty, buried up to her waist in a mound of earth. She is dressed well, if a bit dowdily, and her eyes are closed. A bell rings, shrill and loud, perhaps a message from a cruel God, or at least a mechanistic, indifferent one. It stirs Winnie, as it does us. She opens her eyes and begins to speak compulsively for some thirty to forty minutes, never even trying to extract herself from the earth. She occasionally busies herself by rummaging through her large handbag, taking from it such necessaries as toothbrush and toothpaste, hairbrush and comb, lipstick and mirror, nail file, eyeglasses and magnifying glass, tonic, a music box, and—most surprisingly—a revolver. At various points in her near-nonstop talk she solicits—and sometimes obtains—a response from her husband, who spends most of his time out of our visual field, behind the mound. Although not buried like his wife, he is not entirely mobile, for he is incapable of assuming an upright position. He crawls in and out of a hole, and when we do catch sight of him, he is often behind a newspaper, from which he reads out snippets.

As elsewhere in Beckett the characters bear suggestive names: Winnie and Willie. The most common interpretations point to a certain irony: Winnie, buried in the earth, is hardly the picture of the winner; Willie, little more mobile than his wife, is barely able to assert his will. Together Willie and Winnie resonate as *willy-nilly,* indicating their helplessness. This "real" couple seems no better off than the pseudocouples Vladimir and Estragon, Hamm and Clov.

In the second act things have gone from bad to worse. Now Winnie is buried up to her neck and speaks even more compulsively. The jarring bell rings repeatedly. Her husband manages to crawl entirely around the mound and even a bit up it. Winnie hopes that he is climbing in order to embrace her, but suspects he might be attempting to kill her with the revolver she left out of her bag. Whatever he plans to do, he fails, for he slides down the mound. Winnie, heartened by Willie's momentary nearness, sings a song, as she has promised to do throughout. It is the waltz duet from *The Merry Widow*. On this lyrical note the play ends.

Winnie's positive reaction to Willie's ambiguous ascension shows what an optimist she is. Despite being buried alive, she says toward the beginning of the play: "Can't complain—no no—mustn't complain—so much to be thankful for—no pain—hardly any" (HD 11). Thus the "happy days" spoken of in the title do not refer to some past wistfully evoked; rather the present days are the happy ones.

Winnie is not entirely naïve, for she nuances her view of things: "Oh this *is* a happy day! This will have been another happy day! *(Pause.)* After all. *(Pause.)* So far" (HD 47–48). The pauses suggest she doubts what she is saying herself, and the verb tense ("This *will have been* another happy day") implies that the present is only happy with respect to a future that will be far worse. Strange optimism! Like Malone, who denounces his own story as fiction even while he tells it, Winnie undermines her claim to happiness with the very words she uses to express it.

Winnie finds her greatest happiness when she elicits a reaction, no matter how small, from her generally unresponsive husband. For example, as she wonders whether she should use "it" or "them" to refer to the "hair" or "hairs" on her head, Willie says nothing more than "it." Winnie's response is ecstatic: "Oh you are going to talk to me today, this is going to be a happy day" (HD 23).

It is rumored that Beckett chose a woman protagonist because he wanted the character buried in the earth to possess more objects than could fit into shirt pockets; thus a handbag—and therefore a woman—were necessary. But given the importance of Willie's attention to Winnie, the fact she is a woman seems hardly explainable by the convenience of a large bag. Winnie's prattle corresponds to the kind of language women are expected to produce lest men find them too threatening; her excessive optimism symbolizes the contentedness women are supposed to find in their traditional roles.

Winnie's dependence on Willie is clearest when she has a strange feeling about putting up her parasol. Her uneasiness is justified—in the most spectacular moment in the play the parasol bursts into flames—yet she cannot act in her own behalf without her husband's intervention:

> Bid me put this thing down, Willie, I would obey you instantly, as I have always done, honoured and obeyed. *(Pause.)* Please, Willie. *(Mildly.)* For pity's sake. *(Pause.)* No? *(Pause.)* You can't. *(Pause.)* Well I don't blame you, no, it would ill become me, who cannot move, to blame my Willie because he cannot speak (HD 36).

Winnie's burial in a mound—in Mother Earth—is in many ways symbolic of her femininity. Critics have often compared the mound to a breast. Indeed, in French, the word Beckett uses to designate the mound is "mamelon," related to *mamelle,* meaning breast; and the stage directions specify that Winnie is to have a large bosom. The mound can be compared to another organ: in *How It Is,* Pim's wife "shaved her mound," meaning her vagina (H 76), and Winnie's mound of earth is shaven, insofar as in the torrid heat the ground is scorched and nothing grows on it. In turn Willie, unable to stand erect, would be like a limp penis uselessly moving about the vaginal mound.

Thus Winnie, oppressed like the traditional woman, uses the time-honored arm against her oppressor, throwing into question his potency. She reminds her husband that he is "not the crawler you were, poor darling. *(Pause.)* No, not the crawler I gave my heart to" (HD

46). But Willie does not need to be reminded that he is no longer the man he was. From behind his newspaper he reads out help-wanted ads to which he could not possibly apply: "Opening for smart youth"; "Wanted bright boy" (HD 48). These constitute ironic comments on his own decrepitude, as does his response to Winnie's most insistent question—concerning her toothbrush! Attempting to decipher what is written on its handle, she strains her eyes and reads "genuine pure ... hog's ... setae" (HD 17–18). Comically, she wonders not, as one might expect, what "setae" are (it is Latin for bristles), but rather what a hog is. Willie provides the answer: "Castrated male swine. *(Happy expression appears on Winnie's face.)* Reared for slaughter" (HD 47).

Winnie is happy not only that Willie has spoken to her, not only that he has unwittingly implied that he is as impotent as she, but also because she has learned something. Winnie sets great store by learning, remarking when she first managed to decipher the word *setae:* "That is what I find so wonderful, that not a day goes by—*(smile)*—to speak in the old style—*(smile off)*—hardly a day, without some addition to one's knowledge however trifling" (HD 18). This praise of knowledge is, of course, ludicrous—it is, after all, a question of reading a toothbrush—but it serves to ridicule our belief in progress. We now know that science has not only solved problems but presented new ones such as the possibility of nuclear holocaust, which Beckett examines in *Endgame.* Another paean Winnie addresses to progress rings hollow, dealing, as it does, with sweat:

> I used to perspire freely. *(Pause.)* Now hardly at all. *(Pause.)* The heat is much greater. *(Pause.)* The perspi-

ration much less. *(Pause.)* That is what I find so wonderful. *(Pause.)* The way man adapts himself. *(Pause.)* To changing conditions. (HD 35)

Of course, given the feminist implications of this play, Winnie's speaking of "man's" adaptability in her own case undercuts her words.

In *Happy Days,* Beckett mocks not only science and progress but culture as well. Often when Winnie comes out with a phrase she likes, she punctuates her sentence with the words "the old style." On one occasion she speaks of "the sweet old style" (HD 22). Critics have traced this expression back to Dante's *dolce stil nuovo*—"sweet *new* style."[15] The humanistic enterprise— which has its origins in Dante, the first to write an epic in the vernacular tongue—has run its course by the time we reach Beckett. The fact that concentration-camp guards read Goethe and listened to Bach has shown us that humanistic culture does not render its practitioners humane.

The degradation of culture is depicted in Winnie's fragmented memories of great poets. For example, Ophelia's lines from *Hamlet* (3.1.161–62): "O, woe is me/ To have seen what I have seen, see what I see" are simplified into "woe woe is me [...] to see what I see" (HD 10). Verses from *Paradise Lost* (10.741–42: "O fleeting joys/ Of Paradise, dear bought with lasting woes") fare even worse: "What is that wonderful line? Oh fleeting joys—oh something lasting woe" (HD 14). Moreover, even such imperfect recollection of culture degenerates further; by the end of the play Winnie is not misquoting Dante, Shakespeare, and Milton, but rather Charles Wolfe, a sentimental Irish poet.

We have already noted Winnie's similarities with Malone regarding self-canceling language; she also resembles him in her preoccupation with the fragments of culture that remain to her. Her inspection of the objects in her handbag may remind us of Malone's desire to inventory his possessions, and like him she tells the story of an alter ego. It is that of a child, Mildred, whose nickname, Millie, inverts the initial of Willie. The tale, like most in Beckett, is minimal. Mildred picks up a doll, a mouse runs up her thigh, she drops the doll and screams. Identifying totally with Mildred, Winnie begins to cry out herself. Just enough of a story to evoke the horror of existence, the fear of what Winnie calls "the eternal dark. Black night without end" (HD 60).

These evocations of night contrast with the extreme sunlight in which Winnie is bathed, the "blaze of hellish light" as she calls it (HD 11), perhaps playing upon Milton's "Hail, holy light" (*Paradise Lost* 3.1). In order to bring into relief this unnaturally bright setting Beckett specifies that the backdrop showing the uninterrupted plain and sky be painted in gaudily illusionistic tones ("Very pompier trompe-l'oeil" [HD 7]). Thus it would be the superheated air that makes Winnie's parasol burst into flames. To stop the burning she throws it to the ground, exclaiming, "Ah earth you old extinguisher" (HD 37). In her universe the earth does not foster life but ends it. So unlivable has the environment become that Winnie wonders aloud, "Do you think the earth has lost its atmosphere, Willie?" (HD 51). She finds good in this as she does in everything else: "What a blessing nothing grows, imagine if all this stuff were to start growing" (HD 34).

This end-of-the-world scenario—Winnie and Willie could be the last inhabitants of the planet—suggests a fundamental similarity between this play and *Endgame,* despite obvious differences. One of the refrains in the earlier work was that there is no more of various things: tides, biscuits, pain-killer, etc.; in *Happy Days* Winnie remarks that her lipstick, toothpaste, and tonic are running out. Likewise, she recounts an anecdote concerning the "last human kind [. . .] to stray" by her mound (HD 59), suggesting that people have become as rare a commodity here as in *Endgame.* The passersby Winnie remembers are a couple, unlike her and Willie in that they are erect and ambulatory. The man's reaction to the spectacle of Winnie is heartlessly sexist:

What's she doing [. . .] stuck up to her diddies in the bleeding ground [. . .]? Why doesn't he dig her out? [. . .] What good is she to him like that? (HD 42–43)

Can't have been a bad bosom [. . .] in its day. [. . .] Has she anything on underneath? (HD 58)

Like the unsympathetic spectator of *Happy Days,* the passerby is bewildered by this woman buried up to her breasts. He asks, "What's the idea?" "What does it mean?" "What's it meant to mean?" "No sense in her like that" (HD 42–43). His wife's response is indignant:

And you, she says, what's the idea of you, she says, what are you meant to mean? It is because you're still on your two flat feet, with your old ditty full of tinned muck and changes of underwear, dragging me up and down this fornicating wilderness, coarse creature, fit mate (HD 43).

In other words, by what right do we declare ourselves better than, or different from, the immobile creatures in Beckett's world? Are our powers so much greater than theirs? Is our optimism better founded than Winnie's?

The metatheatrical import of this anecdote is figured in the variants of the couple's name—either Shower or Cooker, as Winnie ill remembers it—which have been interpreted as English reworkings of the German words *Schauer* and *Gucker,* both meaning "looker."[16] Elsewhere Winnie refers explicitly to the "strange feeling that someone is looking at me," that "someone is looking at me still" (HD 40, 49). Thus the situation in which the actress finds herself is analogous to the predicament in which Winnie is caught. They both must go on talking, under their own steam. Winnie gets hardly any response from her husband and is not always sure he can hear her; the actress gets practically no cues from her leading man and must wonder whether she is connecting with her audience.

The correspondence between the actress in need of an audience, passive by definition, and the character dependent on her husband, silent by temperament, emerges perhaps most clearly in these lines:

Ah yes, if only I could hear to be alone, I mean prattle away with not a soul to hear. *(Pause.)* Not that I flatter myself you hear much, no Willie, God forbid. *(Pause.)* Days perhaps when you hear nothing. *(Pause.)* But days too when you answer. *(Pause.)* So that I may say at all times, even when you do not answer and perhaps hear nothing, Something of this is being heard, I am not merely talking to myself, that is in the wilderness, a thing I could never bear to do—for any length of time. *(Pause.)* That is what enables me to go on, go on talking that is (HD 20–21).

The need to "go on," the self-propelling language, reminds us of the Unnamable, but unlike him Winnie suspects that someone is out there, listening to her. The performance of a play entails an immediacy of contact between characters and audience that the reading of a novel does not. There is another difference as well. The object whose attainment Winnie ever puts off is not, as it was for the Unnamable, silence but rather song. Winnie says, in act 1, "Yet it is perhaps a little too soon for my song. *(Pause.)* To sing too soon is a great mistake" (HD 32), and in act 2, "To sing too soon is fatal, I always find" (HD 56). She points to an inevitable "sadness after song," similar to Aristotle's famed "sadness after sexual intercourse" (HD 57).

This difference between silence and song as the object of desire has to do as well with the difference of genre. A novel can only consist of words and the space between them, but a play can have music and movement. The animal sound effects in *All That Fall,* the tape recorder in *Krapp's Last Tape,* the parasol bursting into flames in *Happy Days* show how well Beckett exploits the technical, even the technological, possibilities of theater.

This investigation into the diverse modalities of his media continues as Beckett leaves behind full-length plays and novels, restricting himself to short forms.

NOTES

1. See Ruby Cohn, "Fiction to Theater: *Molloy, The Unnamable, The Lost Ones," Just Play: Beckett's Theater* (Princeton: Princeton University Press, 1980) 219–29.

2. Quoted Cohn, *Samuel Beckett: The Comic Gamut* (New Brunswick, NJ: Rutgers University Press, 1962) 211.

3. Quoted Roy Walker, "Love, Chess and Death," *Twentieth Century* 164 (1958): 537.

4. Theodor W. Adorno, "Towards an Understanding of *Endgame*," trans. Samuel M. Weber, *Twentieth Century Interpretations of* Endgame, ed. Bell Gale Chevigny (Englewood Cliffs, NJ: Prentice-Hall, 1969) 105.

5. Adorno 97.

6. Adorno 86.

7. Beryl S. Fletcher and John Fletcher, *A Student's Guide to the Plays of Samuel Beckett* (London: Faber and Faber, 1985) 102, 107.

8. Pascal, *Thoughts* (Westport, CT: Greenwood Press, 1978) 179.

9. Cohn, *Samuel Beckett* 239.

10. Quoted in Cohn, *Samuel Beckett* 231.

11. Nietzsche, *The Birth of Tragedy and the Case of Wagner*, trans. Walter Kaufmann (New York: Vintage, 1967) 42.

12. Linda Ben-Zvi, *Samuel Beckett* (Boston: Twayne, 1986) 188.

13. Robert Wilcher, "'Out of the Dark': Beckett's Texts for Radio," *Beckett's Later Fiction and Drama,* ed. James Acheson and Kateryna Arthur (Hong Kong: Macmillan, 1987) 5.

14. Quoted Katharine Worth, "Past into Future: *Krapp's Last Tape* to *Breath,"* Acheson and Arthur 21.

15. The network of allusions in *Happy Days* is studied by Cohn, *Samuel Beckett* 253–59; S. E. Gontarski, "Literary Allusions in *Happy Days," On Beckett: Essays and Criticism* (New York: Grove, 1986) 308–24; and James Knowlson, ed., *Happy Days = Oh les beaux jours* (London: Faber and Faber, 1978) 108–11 and passim in the endnotes.

16. Ruby Cohn, *Back to Beckett* (Princeton: Princeton University Press, 1973) 182.

CHAPTER FIVE

Later Works (1961–89)

Given the search for silence in *The Unnamable* and the shortness of breath in *How It Is,* it is not surprising that much of Beckett's output consists of brief works. This is true starting with the poems and critical essays with which he began his literary career, through the French stories he wrote in the 1940s and some of the dramatic pieces he authored in the 1950s (*All That Fall, Krapp's Last Tape, Embers,* and even shorter works such as two mime pieces entitled *Act Without Words I* and *Act Without Words II*). Yet in the '40s and '50s Beckett also composed full-length plays and novels, whereas after 1961 he only wrote short pieces, often under ten pages. It seems as though he imposed an asceticism on himself, much as he did in choosing to write in French.

From 1961 to 1989, Beckett wrote some forty shorter works; therefore, we can only delve into a selection here. Among the dramas we shall study *Play, Film, Breath, Not I, Ghost Trio,* and *Quad;* the prose pieces we shall examine are *Imagination Dead Imagine, Ping, Lessness, For to End Yet Again, Company, Worstward Ho,* and *Stirrings Still.*

Play

This piece, first performed in 1963, features characters even more immobile than the ashcan-dwelling

Nagg and Nell in *Endgame* and the partially buried Winnie in *Happy Days*. *Play* shows us two women and a man, each enclosed in an urn a yard high. Most often they are plunged in darkness, the only illumination coming from a strong beam at the center of the footlights. It is projected onto their faces, usually one at a time, and moves quickly among them. Only when the light is directed at a character does he or she speak.

At the play's beginning the spotlight is projected onto all three. They simultaneously begin to tell their different tales, speaking as they will throughout the play: in "rapid tempo," without emotion, looking straight ahead (csp 147). They seem to have no awareness of each other, but address the "inquisitor" represented by the source of light (csp 158).

The stage then darkens as they stop speaking; soon the light shines on the three again, and they speak together for a shorter time before darkness silences them once more. A few seconds later the light reappears, passing rapidly among them, illuminating now one character, now another, according to no discernible pattern. During each one's several illuminations he or she recounts some incident of the romantic triangle in which they were involved. It is an exceedingly cliché story, told in equally hackneyed terms. For example, the mistress says of the wife: "Her photographs were kind to her. Seeing her now for the first time full length in the flesh I understand why he preferred me" (csp 148).

Some details of this sordid affair: the man promises to go off alone with both his wife and his mistress, but uses professional obligations as a pretext to postpone each departure. The wife has her husband followed, but he buys the investigator off. The mistress is confronted by the wife, once menacingly, once conciliatorily after the man confesses. The whole business ends when the man disappears, and each woman assumes he has run off with the other.

Beckett has said that in *Play* the characters "reflect on their state of being endlessly suspended in limbo."[1] This suggests that theirs is Dantesque punishment: now dead, they are eternally encased in urns, as during their lifetimes they imprisoned others in hopeless relationships. Ironically, the man among them comments, "When first this change I actually thanked God," later adding, "Peace is coming, I thought, after all, at last" (CSP 152). However, death does not bring tranquillity. The mistress says, "I had anticipated something better. More restful" (CSP 152).

In lines reminiscent of the Unnamable wondering what words he must utter to achieve the right to fall silent, the wife asks what she must do to free herself: "Is it that I do not tell the truth, is that it, that someday I may tell the truth at last and then no more light at last, for the truth? (CSP 153). Since there is no indication that the characters are lying, the truth in question must be some larger, not purely factual truth. But while truths can be gotten at, ultimate truth is unattainable, unsayable in all its facets. If they must speak the truth to be released from their punishment, it is clear they will be there forever.

We have seen how in *Waiting for Godot* and *Endgame,* Beckett elaborates mythic situations that last eternally. The same is true of *Play,* which presents toward its end a laconic stage instruction approaching the scandal-ous: "Repeat play" (CSP 157). Everything that has al-ready happened thus happens again, after which yet a second repetition starts! A few seconds later the stage does blacken for good, but that is because the point has already been made: the situation presented in *Play* goes on forever. Hence the irony of the closing words, uttered by the man: "We were not long together" (CSP 158).

Beckett had originally intended the repetition of *Play* to be identical with the first occurrence, but has proposed variations since.[2] For example, he suggests that in the repeat the speed of the characters' speech be increased while the volume is reduced. Thus *Play* would be hurled into a vortex of repetitions even faster and ever fainter, until it escapes our perception. Such a production would have the advantage of justifying *Play*'s ending in the theater as the second repeat be-gins: it is as though it were already fading from our view.

There remains the question of why this play is called *Play*. As the three reflect on their affair, the man says: "I know now, all that was just ... play" and "All this, when will all this have been ... just play?" (CSP 153). He has realized that life was only "play," inessential and empty; he wonders when the sojourn in limbo will also be over and seen as something equally unimportant. The man anticipates this end by viewing the present as already finished, from the perspective of the future, through the use of the future perfect (*"will* all this *have been* ... "*). This was the tense so beloved of Winnie in *Happy Days,* who said repeatedly, "This will have been a happy day."

Yet the word *play* not only connotes the triviality of life and death but also refers to the fact that *Play* is a play. In lines once again reminiscent of Winnie's the mistress poses questions that apply to the actress's situation as well as the character's: "Are you listening to me? Is anyone listening to me? Is anyone looking at me? Is anyone bothering about me at all?" (CSP 154).

Play also merits its title because in content, if not in form, it is the archetypal play. It presents the eternal tale of a marital triangle, done to death by melodramas. Its technique, of course, is far from traditional, but in that sense too *Play* serves as a model. As critic James Knowlson puts it, *"Play* laid the foundations for Beckett's later emphasis on a subtle choreography of sound and silence, light and darkness, movement and stillness."[3] These elements are essential to *Film,* Beckett's only piece written for the cinema.

Film

The opening credits of *Film* (made in New York in 1964) appear against the eye of an old man, whose cracked skin is reptilian; later we realize this is a close-up of the silent-film actor Buster Keaton. This is the only frontal shot we have of him until the end of the twenty-four-minute piece; before then we follow Keaton from behind. Beckett explains in his notes to the screenplay the reason for this strange technique. The character played by Keaton is trying to escape perception, and believes he is not being seen whenever the camera is behind him at less than a forty-five-degree angle. To make this clear, Beckett supplies a diagram:

E stands for the *e*ye of the observer (in the form of the camera), while *O* is the *o*bject being observed (the character played by Keaton). Whenever the camera is within the angle, O does not realized he is being perceived. This device is somewhat naturalistic; it seems normal that when O is followed from behind, he should be unaware of his pursuer, and that he should notice E when E inches toward his field of lateral vision.

Set in the 1920s, *Film* begins with the character scurrying quickly through the streets of an old factory district in order to escape the views of passersby. His haste causes him to run into an old couple; the man is about to hurl abuse at him, but the woman silences her husband with a stage whisper—"sssh" (csp 165). This is the only sound in this otherwise entirely silent piece, and ironically it underscores the muteness.

Keaton enters a building and crouches at the base of a stairwell, avoiding the glance of an old woman coming down. She falls as she reaches the landing, and in her momentary distraction Keaton runs up. He enters an apartment, draws the blinds to block the views of outsiders. In order not to be seen by his pets, he covers goldfish bowl and bird cage, and puts out the dog and cat (in a vaudeville routine where the cat sneaks back every time the dog leaves, and vice versa). He hides a mirror and rips up several photos of himself in order to escape his own view, and he destroys a primitivistic image showing God's face, thereby symbolically shutting out divine awareness. Seemingly perceived now by no one, he seats himself in a rocker and dozes

off, but soon awakens with a start. Now we see him for
the first time from the front; he has a patch over one
eye, and looks out from the other with utter terror.
Following this is another shot, which shows Keaton
staring intently. The fact that the camera is directed
at him for the first time straight on means that he is
painfully aware of being perceived; his being shown
consecutively as observed object (startled from sleep)
and observing subject (staring intently) is meant to
suggest that he is perceiving himself. His having the
use of only one eye reinforces the identification posed
between the lens and the man's viewpoint.

Why the character played by Keaton wishes to escape perception is explained by Beckett in his notes to
the screen play. There he quotes a dictum from George
Berkeley, the eighteenth-century Irish bishop and philosopher: *Esse est percipi,* ("To be is to be perceived").
Beckett elaborates upon these words as follows:

> All extraneous perception suppressed, animal,
> human, divine, self-perception maintains in being.
>
> Search of non-being in flight from extraneous
> perception breaking down in inescapability of self-
> perception.
>
> No truth value attaches to above, regarded as
> of merely structural and dramatic convenience (CSP
> 163).

Beckett pushes the idea "To be is to be perceived" to
the point of meaning "To be is, ultimately, to be perceived by *oneself*," that is, being is self-perception; and
he bases *Film* in philosophical material notwithstanding considerations of truth. This was a strategy he employed in his early novel *Murphy,* whose sixth chapter

shows us not the protagonist's mind as it was but simply as it conceived itself to be.

Would the message of *Film* regarding the inescapability of self-perception be evident in the absence of Beckett's notes? Doubtless not, and that is why some have said *Film* is a failure. However, we may question whether the work is flawed because it depends on outside material for its comprehension. The notion of a totally naïve spectator is a fiction; one always arrives at the movie theater with knowledge about films, with preconceptions and expectations. Even if such innocence were possible, there is no reason to take the unknowing viewer as the ultimate arbiter of art.

Such considerations run counter to the myth of the unity of the work of art, supposedly sufficient in itself. However, even if the viewer knew nothing of the allusion to Berkeley, *Film* would not be devoid of interest. Following Knowlson's formulation quoted at the end of the analysis of *Play, Film* demonstrates Beckett's felicitous interplay of sound and silence (the whisper "sssh" lost in the muteness), light and darkness (thanks to the black-and-white film), and movement and stillness (Keaton's race to the apartment, his deliberate movements to minimize his surroundings, contrast with the frozen shots at the end where he observes himself being observed by himself).

Moreover, *Film* has several memorable moments: the print of God the Father is stark; the cat-and-dog routine is indubitably funny; the rocking chair's curious headrest, with two holes resembling eyes, partakes of the thematics of perception. So does the manila envelope containing the photographs: it is closed by a string attached to two circular holders that look like eyes when it is held sidewise. The 1920s garb of the characters, all old, underscores the fact that *Film* plays upon the idiom of silent movies; the muteness and actions are the same, but gone is the melodramatic thrust. In a frame of French director Jean-Luc Godard's film *Vent d'Est* (1969, *Wind from the East*), we read a caption meaning, "This is not a just image, it's just an image."[4] Accordingly, it might be most useful to consider Beckett's *Film* primarily as a series of images. Hence, perhaps, his title, which suggests that this film about visual perception is the archetypal film.

Breath

No doubt the shortest Beckett work of all is the unclassifiable theater piece *Breath,* first presented in 1969 (CSP 209–11). It consists of no more than a series of sounds we hear while looking at a dimly lit stage strewn with rubbish. First there is the brief cry of a newborn, then a breathing-in (during which the light is increased), then a breathing-out (during which light is decreased), followed by another brief cry. At that point the curtain falls on this play, easily lasting under one minute. As in *Krapp's Last Tape* and *How It Is,* we are in the presence of part-objects: a disembodied cry and rubbish (suggesting excrement).

One can well imagine what wags have said about this work, but such remarks do not negate the boldness of the experiment, its primal significance as a representation of life and death. Beckett uses prelinguistic materials—cries and respiration—to portray the short time we have on this globe. One can view this shortest of plays in relation to the famous lines from *Macbeth:*

"Life's but a walking shadow, a poor player / That struts and frets his hour upon the stage, / And then is heard no more" (5. 5. 24–26). Likewise, critic G. C. Barnard has pointed to *Breath*'s similarity to Pozzo's version of the same thought: "They give birth astride of a grave, the light gleams an instant, then it's night once more" (WFG 57).[5]

Not I

The fragmentation of the body implied by the part-object emerges clearly in one of Beckett's extreme experiments for the theater, *Not I,* first performed in 1972. Onstage the only things visible (and then only in faint light) are, at one end, a mouth and, at the other, a figure of indeterminate sex dressed in a djellabah, the hooded robe worn in North Africa. Beckett calls these characters Mouth and Auditor. The play, which lasts ten to twenty minutes, consists of Mouth's spouting forth sentence fragments, rather rapidly, with shortness of breath. Auditor does nothing except lift his/her arms "in a gesture of helpless compassion" four times in the course of the play (CSP 215).

Mouth's voice is obviously that of a woman, and the words she utters tell of her birth, life, and impending death. The voice is meant to be perceived as a continuum. Before the rise of the curtain we hear it from behind, growing more audible until reaching the volume it will have during the play; after the curtain falls, the voice fades out, but we presume it goes on. It is our imminent departure that renders it imperceptible.

The first words we clearly hear are these: "out . . .

into this world ... this world ... tiny little thing ... before its time ... in a godfor— ... what? ... girl? ... yes ... tiny little girl" (CSP 216). In one of the innumerable moments of self-commentary in Beckett, the first word to come out in *Not I* is *out,* in which we hear the root *ut* of the word *utter* as well as a version of the Latin prefix *ex-,* as in the word *expression.* The speaker literally ex-presses herself, pressing out her words with difficulty, in spurts or spasms; one can compare the production of the words to the childbirth the words speak of. Beckett himself has noted that the illumination of the contracting and expanding mouth alone makes it resemble a vagina.[6] As often in Beckett birth is not a happy event: the world is a "godforsaken hole," and the child comes into it "before its time" (CSP 216).

Though we learn a few lines later that the speaker was an eight-month baby, we need not restrict this evocation of prematurity to its clinical sense. Compared to other species human beings are born in a highly dependent, undeveloped state; the French psychoanalyst Jacques Lacan uses this primordial lack to explain why humans are always in a state of desire.[7] There is a gap between what we are and what we should be, between what we have and what we should have.

Mouth defines her childhood by a lack. Her parents abandoned her, she is unloved:

no love such as normally vented on the ... speechless infant ... in the home ... no ... nor indeed for that matter any of any kind ... no love of any kind ... at any subsequent stage ... so typical affair (CSP 216).

There seems to be an antinomy between the lack of love as a "typical affair" and the unusual circumstances

179

of the child with "no love such as normally vented on the . . . speechless infant." Yet the contradiction is only apparent: the fact that love is "vented" suggests something unsatisfactory about it. As Freud wrote in his article "On Narcissism," the love given to the child is a form of the parent's self-love.[8] The child comes to realize that parental love is not selfless, is not solely intended for it.

The phrase "speechless infant" merits our attention. It is etymologically redundant—*infans* is Latin for "speechless"—and speechlessness is one of the reasons for human premature birth. The child must have several years in which to assimilate the symbolic systems of language and culture, but all does not necessarily proceed well. The accession to the realm of language is an alienating experience: upon the child is imposed a linguistic system made up by generations coming before it. Thus like Mr. and Mrs. Rooney in *All That Fall*, estranged from their own words, Mouth finds herself speaking in "a voice she did not recognize" (CSP 219). And like the Unnamable she cannot control her speech and achieve a desired silence: "can't stop the stream . . . and the whole brain begging . . . something begging in the brain . . . begging the mouth to stop" (CSP 220).

The workings of the pronoun *I* are perhaps the aspect of language that shows most clearly the alienation it entails. We have seen how the Unnamable expresses his trouble with this word, calling it a "whorish" pronoun ("cette putain de première personne" [*L'Innommable* 93]). If anyone can say *I*, then how can I be *I?* To refrain from using the pronoun would be a protest against one's forced insertion into a necessarily alien language; thus Mouth refers to herself exclusively as "she." Four times in the play she comes dangerously close to uttering the forbidden first person, but always keeps herself from falling into its use. About to say *I,* she cries out: "what?..who?..no!..she!" (CSP 217, 219, 221, 222). It is on these occasions that the hooded figure's hands are raised in the "gesture of helpless compassion."

Perhaps the hearer is expressing pity for someone unable to accede to the mastery, illusory as it may be, that use of the first person entails. After all, Mouth's language is aberrant. Although not interrupted by anyone else, her speech constantly alternates with silence, for it is shot through with holes represented by the ellipses between the phrases. Not only a "speechless infant," she was

> speechless all her days ... practically speechless ... how she survived! .. that time in court ... what had she to say for herself ... guilty or not guilty ... stand up woman ... speak up woman ... stood there staring into space (CSP 221).

Mouth's status as victim in a court where she could not speak in her own defense underscores her alienation; the words that urge her to speak—"stand up woman ... speak up woman"—suggest that her oppression and her speechlessness are linked to being female, since the traditional view has it that a woman should be silent. We read in Sophocles' *Ajax:* "'Women should be seen, not heard'—the old, old story."

No less than *Happy Days, Not I* demands a feminist reading. The fact that the child born is a girl appears as something of a surprise, as though it stood to reason that a boy is preferred: "what?.. girl?.. yes ...

tiny little girl" (CSP 216). Like a woman who must make love with selfish men who care not for her enjoyment, Mouth reports that "when clearly intended to be having pleasure . . . she was in fact . . . having none . . . not the slightest" (CSP 217).

Mouth's discontent is also religiously based. She believes that she must suffer according to "that notion of punishment . . . for some sin or other . . . or for the lot . . . or no particular reason" (CSP 217). In conformance with the Catholic doctrine of original sin, reflected in the passage from Calderón's *Life Is a Dream* that Beckett cites in *Proust*—"For man's greatest crime is to have been born" (P 49)—Mouth is being punished for the simple fact of living. She is ironic about God's mercy or even existence, saying she had been "brought up [. . .] to believe . . . with the other waifs . . . in a merciful *(Brief laugh.)* God . . . *(Good laugh.)"* (CSP 217).

Yet suffering because of the simple fact of existence need not be traced only to theological anguish. In a sexist society a woman is oppressed simply because she is a woman, "guilty or not," since in the masculine view that there is "some flaw in her makeup," ill defined though that flaw may be (CSP 221, 218). But let us not pretend that this feminist interpretation, or any other type of reading, can be declared definitive. Mouth warns us against it when she says of "her own thoughts" that she can hardly "make something of them" (CSP 220). Let us not speak in her place; let us not put our words into somebody else's Mouth.

Thus we must question the status of the title, *Not I*. Who utters these words? Clearly not Mouth: whoever cannot say *I* cannot say *not I* either. Is it Beckett, putting the words *not I* into Mouth's mouth—and thus committing the sexist gesture of speaking for the woman, describing her psychology (her inability to say *I*), knowing more about the woman than the woman herself? Perhaps we should attribute these words to the silent hooded figure on stage; perhaps this voice is her/his own, in the form of an estranged mouth representing the alienation inherent in speech.

Ghost Trio

A woman's voice is also important in Beckett's television play *Ghost Trio,* first broadcast by the BBC in 1977. It was the second piece he had written for television; the first was *Eh Joe,* completed in 1965. There are similarities between the two works. Both show a man, a haggard Beckettian down-and-outer, immured in a room—perhaps in a mental institution—with extremely slight furnishings. In neither piece does the man speak, but in each a female voice is heard by the viewer. In *Eh Joe* it is the voice that the character hears inside his head, torturing him with accusatory reminiscences about an unhappy love that his facial expression makes clear he would prefer to forget. The camera moves closer and closer to Joe's face; there is something claustrophobic, histrionic, about the piece.

In *Ghost Trio* all such melodrama is gone, and there is a much greater concern with form. The female voice speaks not to the figure on stage but to the viewers, reminding them that they are watching television:

Good evening. Mine is a faint voice. Kindly tune accordingly. *(Pause.)* Good evening. Mine is a faint voice. Kindly tune accordingly. *(Pause.)* It will not be raised, nor lowered, whatever happens (csp 248).

183

As in *How It Is,* the voice addresses at the very start its own quality, in this case the lack of melodrama: "It will not be raised, nor lowered, whatever happens." The voice goes on to state the obvious, narrating the movements of the camera as it shows us the room from a variety of perspectives: "Look. *(Long pause.)* The familiar chamber. *(Pause.)* At the far end a window. *(Pause.)* On the right the indispensable door" (CSP 248). We see a series of planes and some rectangles: the wall, the floor, the window, the door, the pallet, a cassette tape recorder. Each still shot resembles a Mondrian geometric painting, but executed in black and white: "Colour: none. All grey. Shades of grey" (CSP 248). A television screen is made up of little spots (which project light toward the viewer) against a backdrop of black, so that unlike the warm light of cinema, TV's light is cold; its colors at their most vibrant always are somewhat grey. The highly abstract setting of *Ghost Trio* corresponds to this cold light far better than the pseudorealist and sentimental fictions we usually see on television. Indeed, the word *ghost* functions as an allusion to the medium, insofar as it is the term for the phantom images we see on a malfunctioning TV set. "Ghost" also describes the mere shell of a man, the silent, worn figure in *Ghost Trio,* and is suggestive as well of the disembodied female voice that begins the piece, and of the setting, as empty and inhuman as a ghost town.

The female voice is entirely dispassionate, unlike the voice in *Not I;* this frustrates any sexist expectation we may have that a woman necessarily brings in emotion. Instead, Beckett uses another means to breathe affect into this formalistic world. The voice speaks less and less as the piece goes on; instead, we hear now and again, apparently pouring forth from the cassette recorder the haggard man clutches, fragments of Beethoven's instrumental "Ghost Trio," so called because of its mysterious quality. A rich and melodic piece, it proceeds from an aesthetic diametrically opposed to the one that dictates Beckett's scenario. Yet the fact that the figure is bent over the tape recorder, holding on to it for dear life, suggests a terrible nostalgia for the fullness promised by such art, even if the promise could never be kept. What salvation can be had from art, if the one who clings to it is the pauperized inmate of an institution?

Yet his existence does hold out some hope. Raindrops and footsteps are heard; the man opens the door and finds a little boy in a slicker, come in from the rain. They look at each other for a short time, and the boy turns and goes. The man shuts the door and returns to his listening position. The music crescendos slightly, then there is silence as the camera backs away and the light fades out.

The encounter with the boy perhaps symbolizes the man's recovering his past, his remembering childhood when hope was possible, a nostalgia facilitated by the music. The boy's visit recalls the only evidence of a possible salvation in *Waiting for Godot,* whose both acts end with the arrival of Godot's young messenger. Much as an allegorical painting can tell an entire moral tale through emblems and figures, *Ghost Trio* condenses into a few short minutes the message of *Godot* about the impossibility of hopelessness.

Quad

Beckett's piece *Quad* (1981) is even more abstract than *Ghost Trio*. It shows us four hooded figures, of equal size, who move in rapid rhythm around the edges of a square. Occasionally they approach its center, which they avoid touching as though it were a danger zone. Two versions of *Quad* exist, both filmed for West German television. The first is in color, with various percussion instruments accompanying the figures' movements; the second version is starker, in black and white, with no sound but the bare feet moving across the floor.

Critic Martin Esslin suggests that these figures could be the inhabitants of "a Dantesque hell, doomed to repeat their prescribed circuit to all eternity," or they could represent earthly fate, which causes each of us "to collide with all those whose preordained paths he is preordained to cross at preordained moments."[9] Esslin does well to propose these interpretations merely as possibilities, for the most important thing about this piece is less any meaning one can attach to it than the actual spectacle, the formal, rhythmic use to which the bodies are put. *Quad* is less dramatic than it is choreographic; if music cannot be reduced to any meaning, the same is true of dance.

In a recent article critic Bruno Clément interprets the evolution of Beckett's prose in a way that can allow us to understand the shift in his theater.[10] Clément maintains that starting with *How It Is,* Beckett treats images as earlier he had dealt with voices. The Unnamable felt constrained to speak in a voice that came to him but that he could not claim as his own; the narrator of *How It Is* experiences not only his own voice that way but also certain images. Such were the memories from his sixteenth year, which impinged upon his consciousness only to escape from him no more controllably: "now it's over it's done I've had the image" (H 31).

In his drama as well Beckett displaces his preoccupation with voice onto images. Up to 1961 voice and language have a central importance in his plays, which are at least as narrative as they are visual. Odd though *Waiting for Godot* and *Endgame* may be, their dialogue and plot are as essential to them as the setting, movement, and gestures of the actors; in the radio play *All That Fall* and the tape recorder piece *Krapp's Last Tape,* voice is obviously preeminent. In *Happy Days,* while the image of Winnie in her mound is central, her monologue is an equally necessary component, as are her occasional interactions with Willie.

Contrarily, in many of Beckett's dramatic pieces starting in 1961 narrative and voice assumes less importance. *Film, Breath,* and *Quad* are almost entirely silent, devoid of plot, and dependent on vision for their impact. *Ghost Trio* relies on the interplay of music and silence as much as it does on voice, and has elements reminiscent of abstract and figural painting. Of course, *Play* and *Not I,* which are largely vocal, constitute counterexamples; however, we are arguing the relatively greater importance of images in Beckett's later theater, not their absolute preeminence. Moreover, the image of the characters encased in starkly illuminated urns is a more memorable element of *Play* than the hackneyed story they tell or the orchestration of their voices; and *Not I* owes a good part of its power to the image of the lone mouth cut off from the rest of the body.

Imagination Dead Imagine

The displacement of Beckett's attention from voice onto image is, oddly enough, apparent in certain of his prose works in the '60s and the '70s, despite the necessary presence in all of them of something that can be called narrative voice. Yet voice is not their central concern; rather, images are. In Beckett's work, Clément writes, "elements that are chased out the door come back through the window"; in *The Unnamable,* he asks, "what does the first person mean, if there is no more ego?"[11] The same phenomenon occurs with respect to images in Beckett's *Imagination morte imaginez* (1965, translated as *Imagination Dead Imagine*). We may declare imagination dead, the problem is that a subject has to be there to imagine it so. We may try to rid imagination of all images, conceive it as blank emptiness, but we still end up imagining dead imagination as having a form, perhaps that of a cylinder: "Islands, water, azure, verdure [...] omit. Till all white in the whiteness the rotunda" (FL 63).

The ill has already been done, the imagination has started working again, peopling its universe ever so slightly. Most of *Imagination Dead Imagine* describes the rotunda in extreme detail, though it is never who is seeing it, just as in *The Unnamable* it is never clear who is talking. So objective, so neutral, is the voice in *Imagination Dead Imagine* that at times the text reads like a stage description or a mathematical problem: "Two diameters at right angles AB CD divide the white ground into two semicircles ACB BDA. Lying on the ground two white bodies, each in its semicircle. [...] Go back out, a plain rotunda, all white in the whiteness" (FL 63). The only subject in this text is the implicit *you* of the imperative ("Go back out"). Not the *I* who devised the image, but the *you* who sees it, is the relevant subject, just as the narrator of *The Unnamable* felt himself to be more listener than speaker.

The rotunda described in *Imagination Dead Imagine* is divided into halves, each large enough to accommodate a body lying on its side. The bodies are those of a man and a woman, facing opposite directions. Their backs lie along a diameter, the man's head and woman's buttocks touch one extreme, and the woman's head and man's buttocks are against the other. Their legs are bent, and their knees and feet touch the walls of the rotunda at opposite points. While these two might make us think of homunculi joined in a fertilized ovum, the situation is far more suggestive of barrenness: they are precisely in a position that keeps them from engaging in sex, and thus they function as an emblem for the sterility of the text. The figures remain perfectly still except for an occasional blinking of their left eyes; their right eyes are facing the floor, invisible to the narrator. Since the man and woman are totally white, in a white rotunda, their eyes show a pale blue whose "effect is striking" (FL 65), as the passive narrator tells us. He ends this short piece by telling us that this image is to disappear: "Leave them there, sweating and icy, there is better elsewhere. No, life ends and no, there is nothing elsewhere, and no question now of ever finding again that white speck lost in whiteness" (FL 66). As the image impinged upon the describer without his knowing whence ("The light that makes all so white *no visible source*," FL 63, emphasis added), so it disappears beyond his control. One sees "its whiteness merging in the surrounding whiteness" (FL 65) as the text fades off into the blank page at the end.

Ping

Ping, a Beckett prose piece from 1966, is also organized around an image described in neutral terms. The syntax is even more fragmentary than in *Imagination Dead Imagine;* the phrases, despite an occasional period, are even less sentence-like than the unpunctuated blocks of text in *How It Is.* In *Ping* there are no conjugated verbs, only past and present participles, as though there were no subject imagining but only the object imagined. Given the difficulty of such "midget grammar" (H 76), I have found it useful to add words and punctuation within brackets to certain quotations from this and other late prose works of Beckett; of course, the bracketed elements constitute one possible interpretation among many.

Ping presents to us a white body, erect, with "head haught," "legs joined like sewn," "heels together [at a] right angle," "hands hanging" with "palms [facing] front" (FL 69). The body is in totally white surroundings, so we have the same white-on-white configuration as in *Imagination Dead Imagine.* Once again the sole color is given by the eyes, here of even a paler azure: "light blue almost white" (FL 69). In this static, blank scenario we may feel, as the text has it, that the words constitute "signs [with] no meaning" (FL 69).

However, every so often we come across the word *ping* in sentences that describe some slight change. For example: "Ping murmur only just almost never one

190

second perhaps a meaning" (FL 70). That is to say, for a split second the phenomenon "ping" (wherever it may come from and whatever it may be) introduces a murmur (which is "only just" a murmur, and it "almost never" comes); this murmur brings in "perhaps a meaning."

Once again Beckett brings in through the window what he has chased out the door: "ping" may be the mark of a consciousness in this otherwise empty world. "Ping perhaps not alone" (FL 70): since there is "ping," then maybe the image of the body with legs sewn together is "not alone," it could be part of a larger world. "Ping" could even introduce an entire naturalistic universe and the possibility of memory: "Ping murmur *perhaps a nature* one second almost never *that much memory* almost never" (FL 70, emphasis added). "Ping" goes so far as to offer hope of salvation: "ping perhaps way out" (FL 70). Ping may be the name of God in this text, as Godot seemed to have been in *Waiting for Godot.*

Ping is thus a contradictory piece. On the one hand, imaginative subjectivity seems to be reduced to all but nothing; on the other, the world is reduced to so little that the slight force called "ping" that produces minor changes looms as large as a creator God.

Lessness

The same antinomy occurs in another short prose work by Beckett, *Sans* (1969, translated as *Lessness*). Several critics have described how Beckett composed this piece.[12] He began by devising sixty sentences that repeat elements of each other, so that there is not one sentence that does not include phrases from others; he then put these sentences into a bag and drew them out blindly; that was the order in which they appear in the text. He then divided those sixty sentences into paragraphs of three, four, or five, according to a system he arrived at arbitrarily. Using the same sixty sentences, Beckett repeated the process for the second half of the text, which thus repeats the first half in a different order. Obviously the resultant piece is incredibly repetitious.

There are many things that *Lessness* has less of; one of them would seem to be authorial control. Not only did Beckett allow randomness to come into the creative process, he went so far as to introduce it purposely. This leads us to realize that Beckett is trying to control a certain lack of control; at the precise point where he seems to be reducing the role of consciousness (he does not know what the order of the sentences drawn will be), he is consciously exploiting his lack of consciousness. In a sense he is like Hamm, the king in *Endgame,* who controls what little there is left to control.

Lessness paints a barren world similar to that in *Endgame.* It begins: "Ruins true refuge long last towards which so many false time out of mind" (CSPR 153). Here we see the "lessness" inherent in the reduced grammar; the sentence seems to be saying: "Ruins [are the] true refuge[, at] long last [found,] towards which [one had attempted to go; in the process, one had to go through] so many false [refuges; this search had been going on for] time out of mind [that is, longer than one can remember]." Among the ruins there is the character's "little body [. . . with its] heart beating," the "only upright" thing to be discovered: "[on] all sides [, there is] endlessness" (CSPR 154). This "true refuge" is actually "issueless," that is, there is no way out of it (CSPR 154). It is a refuge from which one cannot take refuge. This place and this character are the sole things existing, not only in space but also in time: there has "never [been anything] but this changelessness" (CSPR 153). As in *Godot* and *Endgame* the world shown us is "timeless": "Never but in vanished dream [has there been] the passing hour" (CSPR 154).

Yet Beckett gives with one hand what he has taken back with the other. In the few sentences with conjugated verbs there is reference to a future—"He will stir in the sand [,] there will be stir in the sky [,] the air [,] the sand" (CSPR 153)—and allusion to a past— "On him will rain again as in the blessed days of blue" (CSPR 155). Critic Susan Brienza does well to remark upon the biblical sound of these sentences.[13] "It will be day and night again over him" (CSPR 154) reminds one of the refrain in the creation story: "And there was evening and there was morning: a first [second, third, etc.] day" (Genesis 1). The impersonal construction "there will be stir in the sky [,] the air [,] the sand" calls to mind God's commandments, "Let there be light" and "Let there be a firmament in the midst of the waters" (Genesis 1: 3, 6). In the Bible, too, there is "lessness": all was "formless and void" before God created (Genesis 1: 2).

But *Lessness* suggests not only creation but also destruction, for its void and formlessness are not so much primordial as the result of some universal catastrophe. This too has its biblical counterpart: the endless ruins remind us of the total destruction that befell Sodom and Gomorrah, and the desolation makes us think of the flood, which is alluded to directly: "He will curse God again as in the blessed days [, with his] face to the open sky [, watching] the passing deluge" (CSPR 153). Indeed, there is something biblical not simply about cursing God, as Job's wife urges him to do, but about cursing per se: we still pray and bless, but we no longer attribute negative power—the power to harm our enemies—to our Gods, or to our words.

Who is this creature, this sole "little body" erect in the desolation? Is he the lone survivor of the catastrophe, a new Noah? That he symbolizes the human species is suggested by the possibility of progress that is attributed to him: "He will live again the space of a step"; "one step more in the endlessness [,] he will make it" (CSPR 154). But we need not try to figure out who he is, or what he is doing: *Imagination Dead Imagine* and *Ping* have taught us to focus on isolated images and settings and not to ask whence they came or where they are going. Indeed, *Lessness* says explicitly that this figure is simply imagined: "Never but silence such that in imagination this wild laughter [,] these cries" (CSPR 154). That is to say, since there has never been anything but silence, we must attribute to imagination "this wild laughter" and "these cries," which might be hyperbolic description of the creature's imprecation of his God.

Likewise, it is pointed out that art is not based on reality: "Never but imagined the blue in a wild imagining the blue celeste of poesy" (CSPR 155). In this black, white, and grey world of *Lessness* blue could only be a figment; where the sky is grey, the heavenly blue one knows from poetry could only be an example of "wild imagining." This idea is a commonplace since baroque times at least: "Nature herself tricks us ... because that blue sky which we all see is neither sky nor blue," wrote the sixteenth-century Spanish poet Bartolomé Leonardo de Argensola.[14]

Beckett pushes to its limit the admission that all here is imagined: "Never but dream the days and nights made of dreams" (CSPR 154). This too is a classical topos, best expressed at the end of the second act of Calderón's play: "Life is a dream, and even dreams are dreams." Yet Beckett once again takes back with one hand what he has given with the other. Even as he accords such importance to dreams, he tells us repeatedly that our fancy is empty: "long last all gone from mind" (CSPR 153). Once more we are to imagine imagination dead.

The title too is a product of the imagination. Beckett coined the word *lessness* to describe his creation not from nothing but from the absence of everything: we must understand the syllable *less* not so much as the opposite of *more* but as the suffix in words such as *meaningless,* where it does not denote less meaning but no meaning at all. In the original French the piece had been called *Sans,* meaning simply "without." When Beckett came up with the English title, he despaired of finding a French equivalent. He worked with essayist E. M. Cioran trying to render the word, but they gave up, claiming "there was no French noun capable of expressing absence in itself, a pure state of absence."[15] If Beckett himself finds his translation more satisfying than the original, this reminds us of the problem posed by his self-translations. Which text is definitive: the one Beckett published in the original language, or the translation to which he may have applied some finishing touches?

For to End Yet Again

In German translations done by Elmar Tophoven in collaboration with Beckett, *Imagination Dead Imagine, Ping,* and *Lessness* were included in a volume called *Residua* (1970), implying that they were what remained of attempts to write longer works. Beckett gave a similar name to his prose text *Fizzles* (1976), suggesting that the pieces in it (written in the 1960s and 1970s) were what remained of larger works that had fizzled out.

The text entitled *For to End Yet Again,* the last "fizzle" in the American edition, starts off like *Imagination Dead Imagine* by presenting a static image: "skull alone in a dark place pent bowed on a board to begin" (F 55). The skull then begins to glimmer, illuminating a scene similar to the one in *Lessness:* all is grey, there are ruins and a solitary figure with a "little body" (F 58). Yet unlike the earlier texts, movement is introduced. Two white dwarfs are sighted afar, carrying a litter face to face and executing steps so synchronized that they appear interchangeable: once again we are in the presence of the pseudocouple. It is not clear what is to be made of these far-off figures in white: against the grey, the narrator tells us, there is "whiteness to decipher" (F 58), a phrase that like "the white speak lost in whiteness" of *Imagination Dead Imagine* refers to the text itself. In this neutral, grey writing, whose object seems on the verge of disappearing, how can we interpret this one surprising element, the presence of the white dwarfs? White on grey does not make for easy reading.

Indeed, the piece ends with the grey light fading gently or switching abruptly (both alternatives are explicit) into "that certain dark that alone certain ashes can [produce]" (F 61). Thus we reach "a last end if ever there had to be another" (F 61). Despite the questioning of ending in the final words, it seems there had to be another end for Beckett. As the title has it, everything was constructed "for to end yet again," to indulge once again in the pleasure of falling silent.

Presentation of images obviously works in painting; we have seen how, in Beckett's later theater, it functions effectively. Yet we may wonder whether he did well to structure prose works around obsessive images, insofar as descriptions tend to serve purposes outside themselves in modern literature. The critic Erich Auerbach has shown how the nineteenth-century French realist Honoré de Balzac used physical description to suggest the "moral atmosphere" of his novels, assigning "sociological and ethical significance" to furniture and clothing.[16] Thus in *Le Père Goriot*, Balzac endows the proprietress of a boardinghouse with an "old, fattish face," "a parrot-beak nose," "small, plump hands," and a "loose, floppy bodice," all of which he says "are in harmony with the room, whose walls ooze misfortune, where speculation cowers."[17]

Critic Roland Barthes points to another function of descriptions in modern literature.[18] They often serve primarily to emphasize the apparently real nature of the story being told: the world presented in the text seems real because it includes diverse objects capable of being inventoried. However, Barthes points out that there have been periods in literary history when description was an artistic end in itself. For example, the second century A.D. knew an excitement for *ekphrasis,* texts whose sole purpose it was to evoke a setting, a moment, a person or a work of art. Beckett's nearly plotless descriptions, which form the substance of much of his prose in the 1960s, may have a pedigree in classical rhetoric, yet they pose an insuperable barrier for many modern readers, who expect at least some form of action in literature. And unlike the ancients, Beckett focuses on the most neutral of images: barren settings and creatures dressed in white. One could argue that the milieus, characters, and plot in Beckett's earlier prose are hardly more varied; however, those texts present action by portraying the inexorable self-propulsion of a voice desperately asking itself what makes it speak.

One may wonder whether Beckett himself was satisfied with his prose focusing on images, for in *Fizzles* he includes along with such pieces others that hark back to the concern with voice in *The Unnamable*. For example, the third piece in *Fizzles, Afar a Bird,* describes hardly any scene at all but recalls the problem that was the basis of *The Unnamable,* the speaker's alienation from the pronoun *I* and the view of the self spoken about as a kind of *he:* "it was he had a life, I didn't have a life"; "he will never say I, because of me" (F 26, 27). As in *Malone Dies,* the *I* wishes to narrate the death of this other, the self to whom *I* only apparently refers: "I'll live his death, the end of his life and then his death, step by step, in the present, how he'll go about it [. . .], it's he will die, I won't die" (F 26–27).

Company

Questions of voice reemerge to the forefront of *Company,* a prose work Beckett published in 1980. This text represents a break with his short, hermetic prose of the 1960s and 70s, for it is somewhat long (56 pages) and straightforward, which is not to say that it makes for easy reading.

As *Company* begins, we are presented with a man lying in the dark, hearing a voice. Who paints this scene is not clear; we are told that all is "devised" (or, translating from Beckett's French version, *imagined, created,* or *invented*), by an unidentified "deviser of the voice and of its hearer and of himself" (c 26). At other points it seems that this "deviser" of the man lying in the dark and of himself is devised by another. This deviser of the deviser, in turn, would be devised by yet another, and so on.

It is not surprising that each deviser is devised by another, insofar as he is also said to be devising himself: to devise oneself, to elaborate one's own identity, implies that there is an agency within oneself, other than oneself, who is doing the devising. In *The Unnamable,* Beckett presented this agency different from the self that creates the self; and in *Company,* Beckett refers to it by its "name," as the "Unnamable." The ultimate deviser of all other devisers is said to be "nowhere to be found. Nowhere to be sought. The unthinkable last of all. Unnamable. Last person. I. Quick leave him" (c 24). This *I,* unnamable, unlocalizable, unassignable to any self, is curiously not the first person but the "last person," the ultimate agency who is hardly a person at all but what makes personhood possible.

There is an important difference between this last person in *The Unnamable* and in *Company.* In the earlier text the *I* speaks for pages on end, constituting its own story, which it should not be able to do: it is a

199

purely speaking *I,* not the *I* spoken of as elaborated self. *Company* offers a critique of that incoherency, for in it the *I* appears only momentarily: "I. Quick leave him." Thus other persons than the first are used to refer to the self:

> He speaks of himself as of another. He says speaking of himself, He speaks of himself as of another (c 26).

> A small boy you come out of Connolly's Stores holding your mother by the hand (c 10).

The passages in the third person are often made up of pronominal acrobatics. In the case above, the first occurrence of the words "He speaks of himself as of another" suggests that a character is being described who refuses to use the pronoun *I;* in the second occurrence— "He says speaking of himself, He speaks of himself as of another"—we realize that it could well be the narrator, speaking of himself, who refuses to use the pronoun *I.* (This becomes clearer if we add the quotation marks Beckett omits: *He says speaking of himself, "He speaks of himself as of another."*) Here we reach a truly monumental creation: a first-person narrative narrated in the third person. "He speaks of himself as of another" literally means *I speak of myself as of another.*

The passages narrated in the second person are remarkable as well. They are recounted by the "deviser" of the man lying in the dark to that man, but insofar as the deviser is said to devise himself as well, the man lying passively in the dark is a figure for the deviser not as self-devising but as self-devised. Thus the passages in the second person—which deal with memories of events having occurred to "you"—show

200

us how the self sees what has happened to it as occurring to another. The self that remembers is different from the self remembered; yet what occurred to the self one used to be has also happened to the self one is now: "In the end you will utter again. Yes I remember. That was I. That was I then" (c 21).

The factitiousness of the process whereby one assumes one's past is clear when we consider that we know about our own birth. To say, *I was born on such and such a day,* implies that one can know such a fact for sure; by rights one should say, *I was told I was born on such and such a day,* or *I was told, "You were born on such and such a day."* Thus Beckett writes in *Company,* "You were born on an Easter Friday after long labour. Yes I remember" (c 34). The words "I remember," absurd insofar as one cannot "remember" one's birth, point to the gap existing between the *I* that remembers and the *I* that is remembered.

This passage becomes more interesting when we learn that Beckett himself was born on the Friday before Easter. Moreover, other events *Company* recounts in the second person occurred to Beckett himself;[19] thus our author believes his own identity to be as factitious as his characters'. When we saw that each deviser in *Company* was devised by another, we might have felt that this infinite chain of devised devisers must end in the person of Samuel Beckett. Yet Beckett makes it clear here that he is not the ultimate point of reference and that the source of the voice that emerges from him is an enigma for himself. Even he does not know who is devising the autobiographical self presented in *Company*.

This text is so named because it sees this otherness

201

within the self, the otherness of one's own voice and memories, as a source of companionship. The narrator is a "deviser of himself for company," his deviser is "another devising it all for company," each is a "devised deviser devising it all for company" (c 26, 33, 46). And should we find all of this hard to follow, we are told, "Confusion too is company up to a point" (c 26). In fact, such company may be more satisfying than that furnished by others. In the autobiographical passages of the text the mother emerges as punishing, the father as distant, and the lover as unresponsive.

Of course, the company one provides oneself is hollow, but one keeps this realization at bay: "You do not murmur in so many words, I know this doomed to fail and yet persist" (c 61). Rather, failure too is seen as occurring to another: "You view yourself to this effect as you would a stranger suffering say from Hodgkin's disease or if you prefer Percival Pott's surprised at prayer" (c 61). One prays to God, the ultimate Deviser of company, like the *I* in that he is "unnamable," "unthinkable," and "nowhere to be found" (c 24). Yet prayer promises little success: remember that Clov in *Endgame* said of God, "The bastard. He doesn't exist!"

Others had turned out to be disappointing company, God is "nowhere to be found," and oneself as a source of company is a questionable prospect. Failure is inevitable, yet the book's final words find comfort in that:

And how better in the end labour lost and silence. And you as you always were.

Alone.

202

Once again a Beckettian narrator achieves a desired silence, but there is a coda: the realization that one is and has always been alone. Yet although the text ends here, it is like *The Unnamable* in that is goes on after its close. Company—and *Company*—continue in the awareness of solitude, in the silence, because being conscious of oneself as alone implies that one sees oneself alone, that one sees oneself as another alone. One is thus doubled again into self-deviser and self-devised. There is a curious optimism here: one is never quite as alone as one thinks, precisely because one thinks. In thinking one invents oneself as another. Descartes said, "I think, therefore I am"; Beckett says, *I think, therefore I keep myself company.*

Worstward Ho

If *Company* found comfort in failure, *Worstward Ho* (1983) rejoices in it. Playing on the title of Charles Kingsley's 1855 novel *Westward Ho!* describing the British Empire's self-confident expansion, *Worstward Ho* bespeaks Beckett's assured march not toward the west but toward the worst. *Worstward Ho* also resonates as *worstWORD ho,* urging us on to the worst *word.* Thus it takes as its point of departure the inevitability of failure: our speech is always flawed. We read on the first page: "say for be missaid." This expression suggests we shall see the word *say,* there will seem to be a narrator claiming he *says* things, when things are simply *being said* or *missaid,* by whom we cannot know.

What is being ill said concerns only fleeting images, of the kind Beckett has offered us since the first pages of *How It Is.* Here is an example: "Say a body.

Where none" (WH 7). What is presented is not only fictional, it is not even real in the fictional world. Later we learn that this nonexistent body is kneeling. Other images that emerge and fade throughout the book are a head, a couple made up of an old man and a child, and toward the end a woman.

However, the real force of *Worstward Ho* resides not in these intermittent images but in the ironic voice that presents them. For example: "In the dim void bit by bit an old man and child. Any other would do as ill" (WH 13). Thus the picture of the old man and boy is conjured up not because it is no worse than other images, but because it is no better. When one has realized that there is no way to say anything well, one resigns oneself to speaking badly: "Try again. Fail again. Fail better" (WH 7). A perverse delight is taken in failure; if one makes a virtue of the necessity of failing, doing worse actually means doing better—which comes to mean one does well in spite of oneself.

Fulfilling the desire to do ever worse is contradictory in another way: one can only go "worst*ward*," toward the worst, without hope of attaining it. For what is worse: the worst, or what is almost the worst? The almost-the-worst is less perfect, and therefore worse than the worst. For in its perfect badness the worst would be tainted by the "want of flaw" (WH 44); it would be "the worst in need of worse" (WH 31). Thus as we go "worstward," toward the truly worst, the imperfect worst, we end up avoiding the worst of all! "No future in this. Alas yes" (WH 10). Such words convey a curious optimism: "How almost true they sometimes almost ring! How wanting in inanity!" (WH 21).

Inanity—emptiness, senselessness—is lacking, because meaning attaches to these words despite everything. We have seen how several of Beckett's later texts, try as they might to eradicate all subjectivity, always end up bringing it back in. *Imagination Dead Imagine* says in its title that one needs imagination to envisage dead imagination; *Ping* is the sound that marks consciousness in an otherwise empty world; *Lessness* tries to control the author's lack of subjective control. It is as though, after showing us the absurdity of life in *Waiting for Godot* and *Endgame,* Beckett wished to push meaninglessness to the limit in the apparently purposeless texts he started writing in the 1960s, only to show us that consummate absurdity is "wanting in inanity." This is because for something to be truly absurd, a standard of nonabsurdity—in the form of an organized consciousness—is needed in order for the absurd to take on relief as the absurd. Adorno had written of *Endgame* that one has to comprehend its incomprehensibility, but that too is something to comprehend.

One can say of Beckett's latest works, written in the strangest French and English, what literary theorist Walter Benjamin wrote of the German poet Friedrich Hölderlin's eccentric translations from Sophocles: "In them meaning plunges from abyss to abyss until it threatens to become lost in the bottomless depths of language. There is, however, a stop."[20] Sense may move toward extinction, but it can never be totally undone.

Stirrings Still

Even death does not exist for us as pure nothingness but rather in reference to something—life—that it is not. Death is something other than life, which means that it *is* something. "Oh how something," as Beckett put it in *Stirrings Still* (1988), the last text he published.[21]

This short prose piece begins by showing us a man seated at his table, head in hands; we presume he may have been writing. Like Malone telling the story of Macmann, or the narrator of *Company* evoking his past, he seems to be speaking of himself in the third person. We find in him the familiar Beckett vagabond, wearing the "same hat and coat as of the old when he walked the roads."

This man is waiting for death, even desiring it: "Oh to end. No matter how no matter where. Time and grief and self so called. Oh all to end." Yet death has a nasty habit of not coming when we expect it. We may think it is about to arrive, but it does not: "Perhaps thus the end. Unless no more than a mere lull. Then all as before. [. . .] So again and again. And patience till the one true end to time and grief and self."

Yet such patience does little good. We are "waiting for nothing again," we are waiting for the nothing that death is, as we waited for Godot, fruitlessly. As was noted on the first page of this study, our encounter with death is a missed one, for we are dead to death when it has arrived. Indeed, waiting for death is "waiting for nothing," waiting to no purpose.

The fact that death is unattainable is suggested by the title, with its many resonances. No matter how old we are, no matter how close to death, we are *stirring still*—still alive. When we imagine ourselves dead—"still" in the sense of quiet—we are stirring even in

206

our stillness, for we see ourselves as *being* dead. This has its good and bad sides: "No danger or hope as the case might be of [. . .] ever getting out of it."

Thus we can hardly foresee death—"so on unknowing no end in sight"—and we presume that Beckett did not knowingly encounter death. His narrator in *Stirrings Still* speaks of a man "Darly [who] once died and left him," yet the author of *Malone Dies* could never say that he himself had died, for the utterance *I die* is impossible. Instead, he illustrated throughout his works that the speaking *I* can never die, and therein lies his immortality. Thus though he is dead, Beckett's words stir us still.

NOTES

1. Quoted Beryl S. Fletcher and John Fletcher, eds., *A Student's Guide to the Plays of Samuel Beckett* (London: Faber and Faber, 1985) 185–86.

2. Fletcher and Fletcher 186.

3. James Knowlson, "Drama After *Endgame*," Knowlson and Pilling, *Frescoes of the Skull* (New York: Grove, 1980) 112.

4. "Ce n'est pas une image juste, c'est juste une image"; frame reproduced in Colin MacCabe, *Godard: Images, Sounds, Politics* (Bloomington: Indiana University Press, 1980) 62; my translation.

5. G. C. Barnard, quoted Fletcher and Fletcher 209.

6. Knowlson, "Ends and Odds in Drama," Knowlson and Pilling, 200.

7. Jacques Lacan, *Ecrits* (Paris: Editions du Seuil, 1966) 96, 98.

8. Freud, "On Narcissism," *Standard Edition* 14: 90–91.

9. Martin Esslin, "Towards the Zero of Language," *Beckett's Later Fiction and Drama,* ed. James Acheson and Kateryna Arthur (Hong Kong: Macmillan, 1987) 44.

10. Bruno Clément, "Les Yeux fermés (la poétique imaginaire de Samuel Beckett)," *Les Temps Modernes* 509 (1988): 160–71.

11. Clément 166; my translation.

12. See, e.g., Ruby Cohn, *Back to Beckett* (Princeton: Princeton University Press, 1973) 262–67, and Susan Brienza, *Samuel Beckett's New Worlds* (Norman: University of Oklahoma Press, 1987) 179–80.

13. Brienza 187–88.

14. In Elias L. Rivers, ed., *Renaissance and Baroque Poetry of Spain* (New York: Scribner's, 1966) 153.

15. E. M. Cioran, "Quelques rencontres," *Samuel Beckett,* ed. Tom Bishop and Raymond Federman (Paris: Editions de l'Herne, 1976) 103; my translation.

16. Erich Auerbach, *Mimesis*, trans. Willard R. Trask (Princeton: Princeton University Press, 1953) 468, 471.

17. Quoted from translation in Auerbach 469.

18. Roland Barthes, "L'Effet de réel," in Barthes et al., *Littérature et réalité* (Paris: Editions du Seuil, 1982) 81–90.

19. See, e.g., Linda Ben-Zvi, *Samuel Beckett* (Boston: Twayne, 1986) 9–10, and Alfred Simon, *Beckett* (Paris: Belfond, 1983) 270.

20. Walter Benjamin, "The Task of the Translator," *Illuminations,* trans. Harry Zohn (New York: Schocken, 1969) 82.

21. Samuel Beckett, *Stirrings Still* (New York: Blue Moon, 1988). Because this text is unpaginated and short, the quotations from it here are not accompanied by references.

BIBLIOGRAPHY

Works by Beckett (limited to texts from which the present study quotes)

English Editions

All published by Grove Press, New York, unless otherwise noted. An asterisk after the title means that Beckett originally wrote the work in French and translated it himself.

Company, 1980.

Collected Poems in English and French, 1977. Includes original poems in both languages, Beckett's translations of these and of French poems by other writers.

Collected Shorter Plays of Samuel Beckett, 1984. Some pieces originally in English, some translated from the French.

Collected Shorter Prose 1945–1908. London: John Calder, 1984. Some pieces originally in English, some translated from the French.

Disjecta: Miscellaneous Writings and a Dramatic Fragment. Ed. Ruby Cohn, 1984. Some pieces originally in English, others translated from the French.

*Endgame,** 1958.

First Love and Other Shorts, 1974. Some pieces originally in English, others translated from the French.

Fizzles, 1976. Some pieces originally in English, some translated from the French.

Happy Days, 1961.

*How It Is,** 1964.

*Ill Seen Ill Said,** 1981.

*Mercier and Camier,** 1974.

More Pricks than Kicks, 1970.

Murphy, 1957.

Proust, 1957.

Stirrings Still. New York: Blue Moon, 1988.

Stories and Texts for Nothing, 1967. All pieces translated from the French by Beckett alone except "The Expelled" and "The End," translated by Beckett along with Richard Seaver.

Three Novels by Samuel Beckett, 1965. Includes *Molloy,* translated by Beckett along with Patrick Bowles, *Malone Dies,** and *The Unnamable.**

Waiting for Godot,* 1954.

Watt, 1953.

Worstward Ho, 1983.

French Editions

All published by Editions de Minuit, Paris. Quotations in the present study are from the most recent printings.

L'Innommable, 1951. New printing with different pagination, 1971. Translated as *The Unnamable.*

Molloy, 1951. Collection "Double," 1982. Translated as *Molloy.*

Malone meurt, 1951. New printing with different pagination, 1971. Translated as *Malone Dies.*

Other Editions

Happy Days = Oh les beaux jours. Ed. James Knowlson. London: Faber and Faber, 1978. Features, on facing pages, the original English text and Beckett's French translation, as well as copious notes by Knowlson in the prefatory and final sections.

Residua: Prosadichtungen in drei Sprachen. Frankfurt am Main: Suhrkamp, 1970. This volume includes Beckett's French originals and English translations of *Enough, Imagination*

Dead Imagine, Ping, and *Lessness,* as well as German versions done by Elmar Tophoven in collaboration with Beckett.

Translation by Beckett

Anthology of Mexican Poetry. Comp. by Octavio Paz. Bloomington: Indiana University Press, 1958.

Works about Beckett

Given the volume of criticism on Beckett, we include here only the works that were most useful in writing the present book and that may be of greatest help to the beginning reader of Beckett.

English Works by One Author or Collaborators

Bair, Deirdre. *Samuel Beckett: A Biography.* New York: Harcourt Brace, 1978. So complete that Beckett is rumored to have said, "Deirdre Bair knows more about me than I do." So indiscreet that Bair admits, "I am sure he did not want this book to be written and would have been grateful if I had abandoned it" (xii).

Ben-Zvi, Linda. *Samuel Beckett.* Boston: Twayne, 1986. Includes basic summaries of all of Beckett's works and some interpretation.

Brienza, Susan. *Samuel Beckett's New Worlds.* Norman: University of Oklahoma Press, 1987. Exceedingly attentive readings of Beckett's later fiction, good explication of his "midget grammar." Unfortunately, we are consistently told that Beckett's work is "beautiful," with no explanation of that label.

Coe, Richard. *Samuel Beckett.* Rev. ed. New York: Grove Press, 1968. Traces Beckett's debt to various religions and philosophies, Eastern and Western.

Cohn, Ruby, *Samuel Beckett: The Comic Gamut*. New Brunswick, NJ: Rutgers University Press, 1962. One of the first books on Beckett, it places him within various comic traditions. Cohn's other books are less focused but full of information.

———. *Back to Beckett* (Princeton: Princeton University Press, 1973).

———. *Just Play: Beckett's Theater* (Princeton: Princeton University Press, 1980).

Connor, Steven. *Samuel Beckett: Repetition, Theory and Text*. Oxford: Basil Blackwell, 1988. Subtle analysis of repetition and self-translation in Beckett, using theories of French philosophers Gilles Deleuze and Jacques Derrida.

Fletcher, Beryl S., and John Fletcher. *A Student's Guide to the Plays of Samuel Beckett*. 2d rev. ed. London: Faber and Faber, 1985. This marvelously organized volume is full of information and diverse interpretations of all Beckett's plays.

Fletcher, John. *The Novels of Samuel Beckett*. London: Chatto and Windus, 1964. Basic, sensitive exegesis of the novels.

———. *Samuel Beckett's Art*. London: Chatto and Windus, 1967. Extends the analysis to Beckett's plays and criticism, and includes interesting chapters on Beckett's French and his relationship to philosophy.

Kenner, Hugh. *Samuel Beckett: A Critical Study*. New rev. ed. Berkeley: University of California Press, 1968. An expository treatment of Beckett's writings, including the marvelous reading of Molloy's bicycle discussed in chapter 3 above.

———. *A Reader's Guide to Samuel Beckett*. New York: Farrar, Straus, 1973. Contains an interpretation of *Waiting for Godot* as reflecting life in France under the German occupation.

Knowlson, James, and John Pilling. *Frescoes of the Skull: The Later Prose and Drama of Samuel Beckett*. New York: Grove Press, 1980. Close readings of Beckett's later works, more theoretically sophisticated than Ben-Zvi's or Brienza's, but somewhat long-winded.

French Works by One Author

Bernal, Olga. *Langage et fiction dans le roman de Beckett.* Paris: Gallimard, 1969. In the best piece of theoretically based criticism of Beckett, Bernal places him squarely within the investigation of language started in France by readers of Heidegger.

Janvier, Ludovic. *Pour Samuel Beckett.* Paris: Editions de Minuit, 1966. A Heideggerian reading of Beckett's work, less rigorous but more suggestive than Bernal's.

————. *Samuel Beckett par lui-même.* Paris: Editions du Seuil, coll. Ecrivains de toujours, 1969. An essayistic catalogue of themes in Beckett.

Simon, Alfred. *Beckett.* Paris: Belfond, 1983. Includes summaries of all of Beckett's works and some interesting remarks on his bilingualism.

English Collections of Articles on Beckett

Acheson, James, and Kateryna Arthur, eds. *Beckett's Later Fiction and Drama: Texts for Company.* Hong Kong: Macmillan, 1987. The most interesting collection on the recent works, including much information on the production of Beckett's minimalist drama.

Chevigny, Bell Gale, ed. *Twentieth Century Interpretations of* Endgame. Englewood Cliffs, NJ: Prentice-Hall, 1969. Features the important piece by Theodor Adorno, the social theorist of the Frankfurt school.

Cohn, Ruby, ed. *Casebook on* Waiting for Godot. New York: Grove Press, 1967. Includes some of the first reviews of Beckett's best-known work. A similar, more recent volume edited by Cohn, *Samuel Beckett: Waiting for Godot: A Casebook* (Hong Kong: Macmillan, 1987), has far less early material.

Gontarski, S. E., ed. *On Beckett: Essays and Criticism.* New

York: Grove Press, 1986. Contains articles on diverse aspects of Beckett's work, including the production of his plays. The most accessible reprint of the translations of the important articles by the French novelists Georges Bataille and Maurice Blanchot. J. E. Dearlove's article pinpoints differences between *How It Is* and earlier works by Beckett.

Graver, Lawrence, and Raymond Federman, eds. *Samuel Beckett: The Critical Heritage*. London: Routledge and Kegan Paul, 1979. An interesting volume that features many first reviews of Beckett's works, including American novelist John Updike's parody of *How It Is*.

French Collections of Articles on Beckett

Bishop, Tom, and Raymond Federman, eds. *Samuel Beckett*. Paris: Editions de l'Herne, 1976. A large collection of diverse pieces: Beckett works with manuscript variants, biographical essays, and critical studies.

Nores, Dominique, ed. *Les Critiques de notre temps et Beckett*. Paris: Garnier Frères, 1971. Includes excerpts from a wide variety of French and foreign works on Beckett.

Rabaté, Jean-Michel, ed. *Beckett avant Beckett: Essais sur le jeune Beckett (1930–1945)*. Paris: Presses de l'Ecole Normale Supérieure, 1984. This collection of theoretical articles is the best volume on Beckett's early writings.

Bibliography

Federman, Raymond, and John Fletcher. *Samuel Beckett: His Works and Critics*. Berkeley: University of California Press, 1970. Exhaustive up to the date of publication. Many of the later books listed above contain substantial, but less complete, bibliographies that could supplement this one.

English Articles and Chapters in Books

"Beckett's Letters on *Endgame:* Extracts from His Correspondence with Director Alan Schneider." *Village Voice* 19 Mar. 1958: 8, 15. Includes reflections on play production and the "wastes and wilds of self-translation."

Esslin, Martin. "Introduction: The Absurdity of the Absurd" and "Samuel Beckett: The Search for the Self." *The Theatre of the Absurd.* Rev. ed. Woodstock, NY: Overlook Press, 1973. 1–65. Points out the difference between absurdity in Sartre and Camus and absurdity in Beckett.

Walker, Roy. "Love, Chess and Death." *Twentieth Century* 164 (1958): 533–44. Contains Beckett's important remark on the two thieves crucified with Jesus.

French Articles

Clément, Bruno, "Les Yeux fermés (la poétique imaginaire de Samuel Beckett)." *Les Temps Modernes* 509 (1988): 160–71. This piece offers a new way to envisage the shift in Beckett's writing that started with *How It Is.*

Rey, Jean-Michel. "Sur Samuel Beckett." *Café Librairie* 1 (1983): 63–66. Includes interesting remarks on Beckett's French.

Other Relevant Works

Auerbach, Erich. *Mimesis: The Representation of Reality in Western Literature.* Trans. Willard R. Trask. Princeton: Princeton University Press, 1953.

Barthes, Roland et al. *Littérature et réalité.* Paris: Editions du Seuil, 1982.

Benjamin, Walter. *Illuminations.* Trans. Harry Zohn. New York: Schocken, 1969.

Camus, Albert. *The Stranger.* Trans. Stuart Gilbert. New York: Knopf, 1946.

Descartes, René. *Discourse on Method and Meditations on First Philosophy*. Trans,. Donald A. Cress. Indianapolis: Hackett, 1980.

Freud, Sigmund. *The Standard Edition of the Complete Psychological Works*. Trans. James Strachey et al. London: Hogarth, 1953–73.

Joyce, James. *Finnegans Wake*. New York: Viking Press, 1939.
———. *Ulysses*. Corrected ed. by Hans Walter Gabler et al. New York: Random House, 1984.

Lacan, Jacques. *Ecrits*. Paris: Editions du Seuil, coll. Le Champ freudien, 1966.

Sartre, Jean-Paul. *Being and Nothingness*. Trans. Hazel E. Barnes. New York: Philosophical Library, 1956.
———. "Orphée noir." *Anthologie de la nouvelle poésie nègre et malgache de langue française,* ed. Léopold Sédar Senghor. Paris: Presses Universitares de France, 1948.
———. *Sartre on Theater*. Comp. and ed. Michel Contat and Michel Rybalka. Trans. Frank Jellinek. New York: Pantheon, 1976.